HOW TO DRAW
MANGA

Edited by Lara Murphy
Designed by Jake Da'Costa
Cover design by John Bigwood

Illustrated by Jolene Yeo
and Shirley Tan at
Collateral Damage Studios

First published in Great Britain in 2024 by LOM ART,
an imprint of Michael O'Mara Books Limited,
9 Lion Yard, Tremadoc Road, London SW4 7NQ

W www.mombooks.com/lom   Michael O'Mara Books   @OMaraBooks   @lomart.books

Illustrations and layouts © Michael O'Mara Books Limited 2024

A CIP catalogue record for this book is available from the British Library.

ISBN: 978-1-915751-02-7

1 3 5 7 9 10 8 6 4 2

This book was printed in China.

HOW TO DRAW MANGA

LOM ART

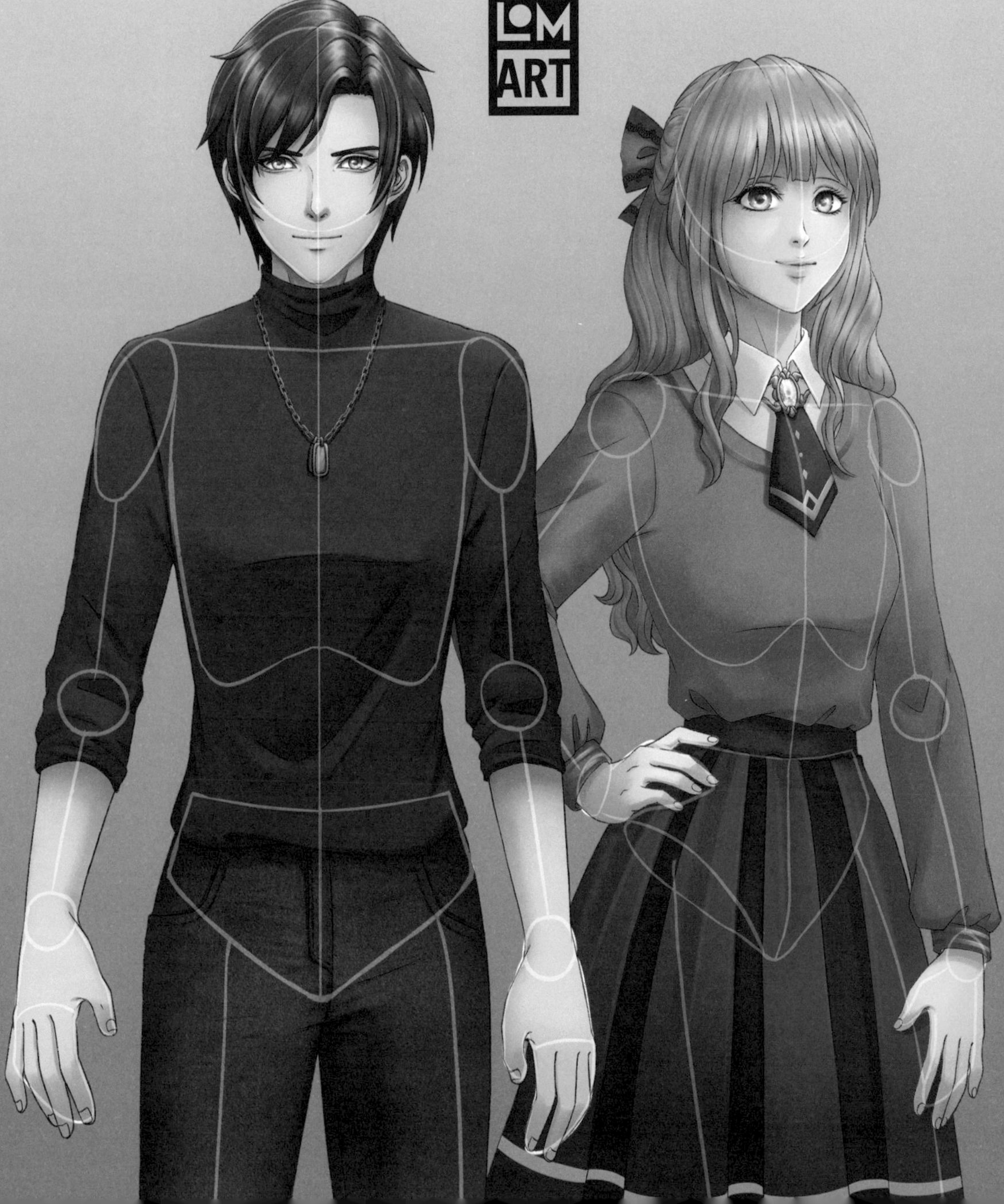

INTRODUCTION

From the blank page to a finished masterpiece, this book provides all the information you need to draw an eclectic range of manga characters. With a focus on popular Shonen manga, learn how to craft dynamic characters that conform to classic manga conventions. For cuter characters, experiment with the adorable Chibi style; both styles are featured within these pages.

Begin by perfecting the basics: heads, hairstyles, facial features and expressions. Move on to body shapes and proportions, then progress to more active poses and complex characters. Use your imagination to add unique accessories, outfits and dramatic special effects. From wicked vampire knights to sweet folklore creatures and dystopian cyborgs, the opportunities for character design are endless.

Let your imagination run wild and draw when the impulse strikes – you never know when your next character or story will pop into your head.

ABOUT THE ARTISTS

Jolene Yeo

Jolene Yeo is a Resident Artist at Collateral Damage Studios in Singapore. She graduated from 3dsense Media School, having studied Concept Design and Illustration. Her dream of becoming an illustrator started when she was very young, and she now works in both 2D and 3D art styles.

Shirley Tan

Shirley Tan is a concept designer and illustrator based in Singapore. She loves drawing beautiful characters and whimsical settings. She is always looking to design fun, inspiring and memorable creative work.

CONTENTS

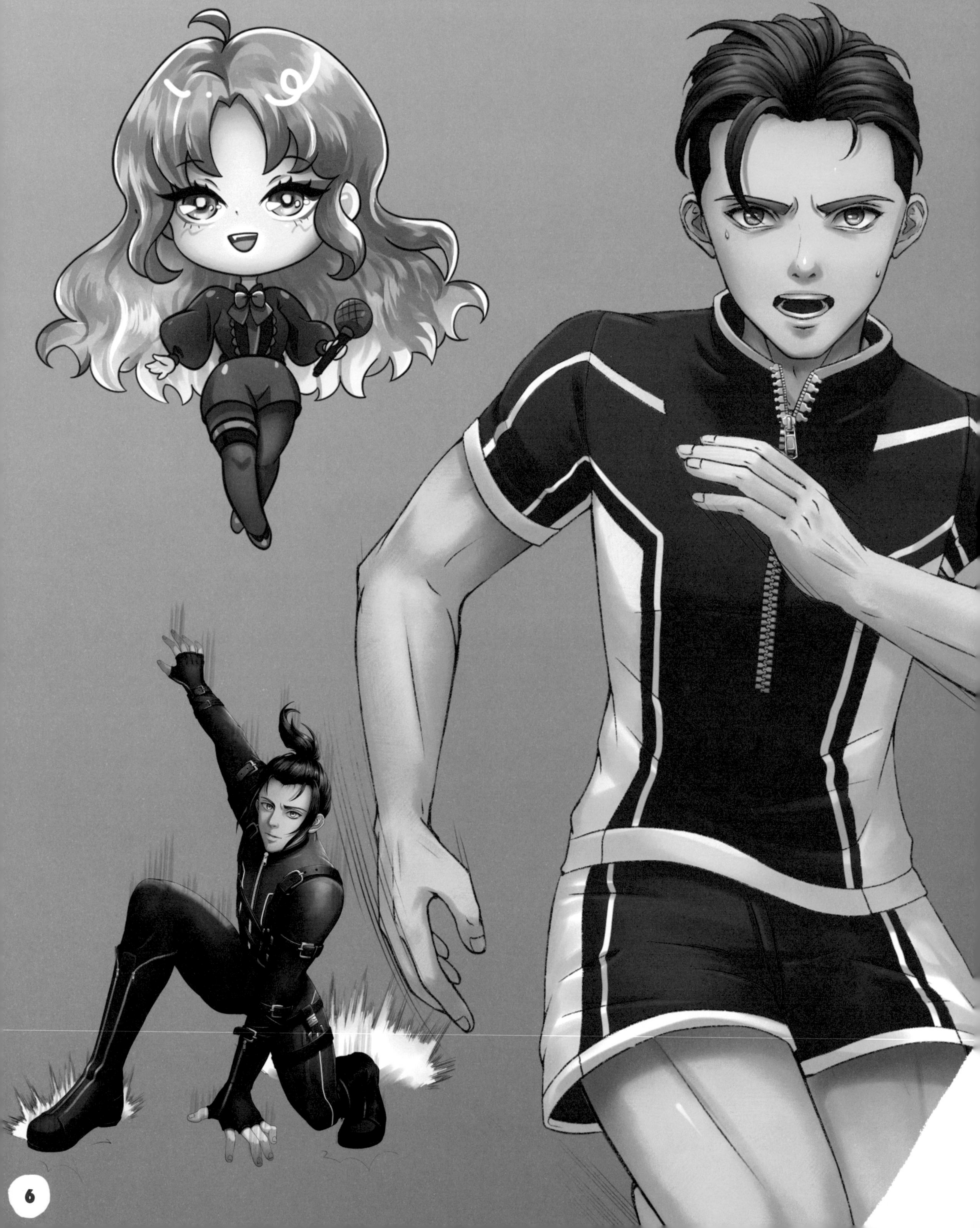

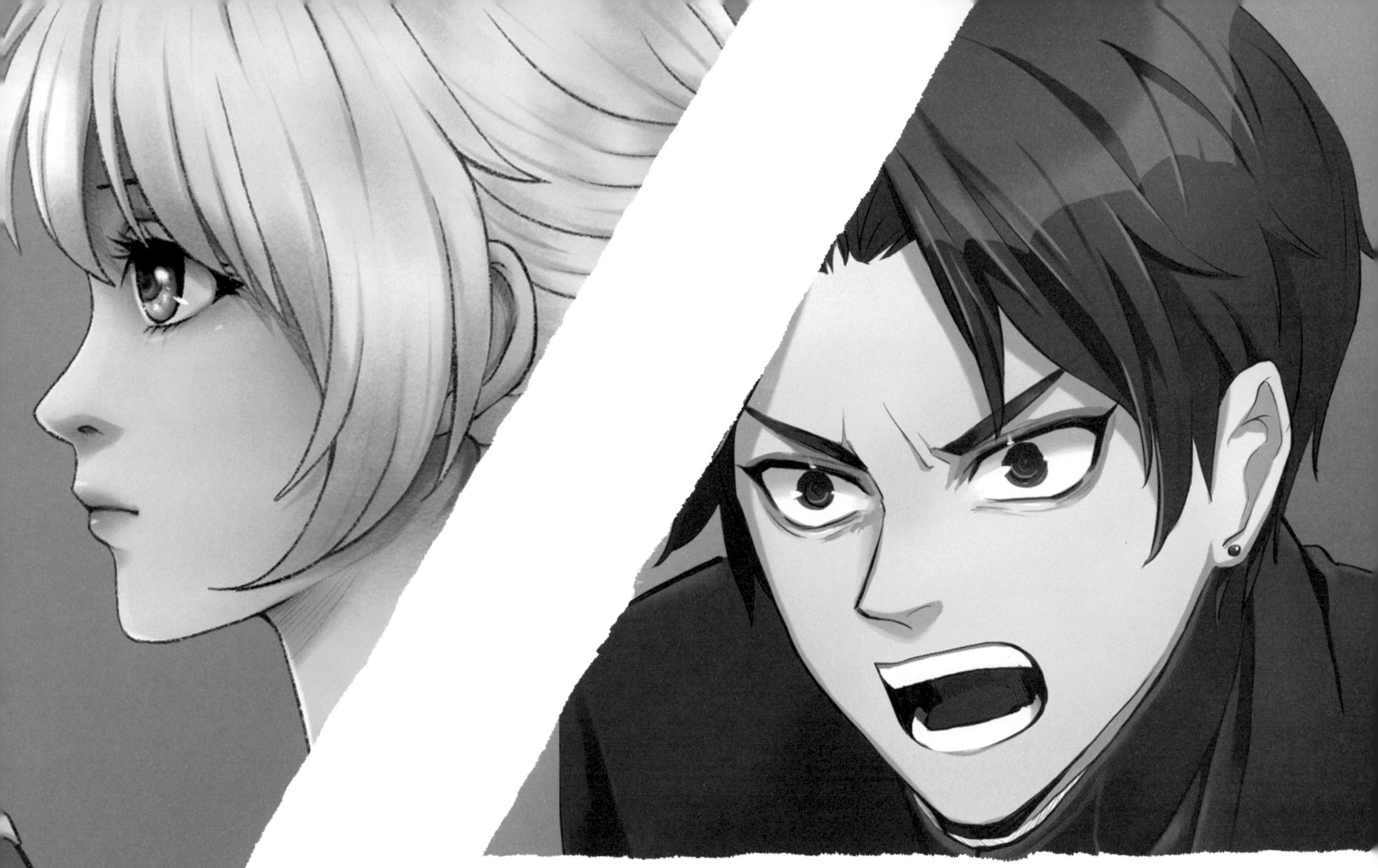

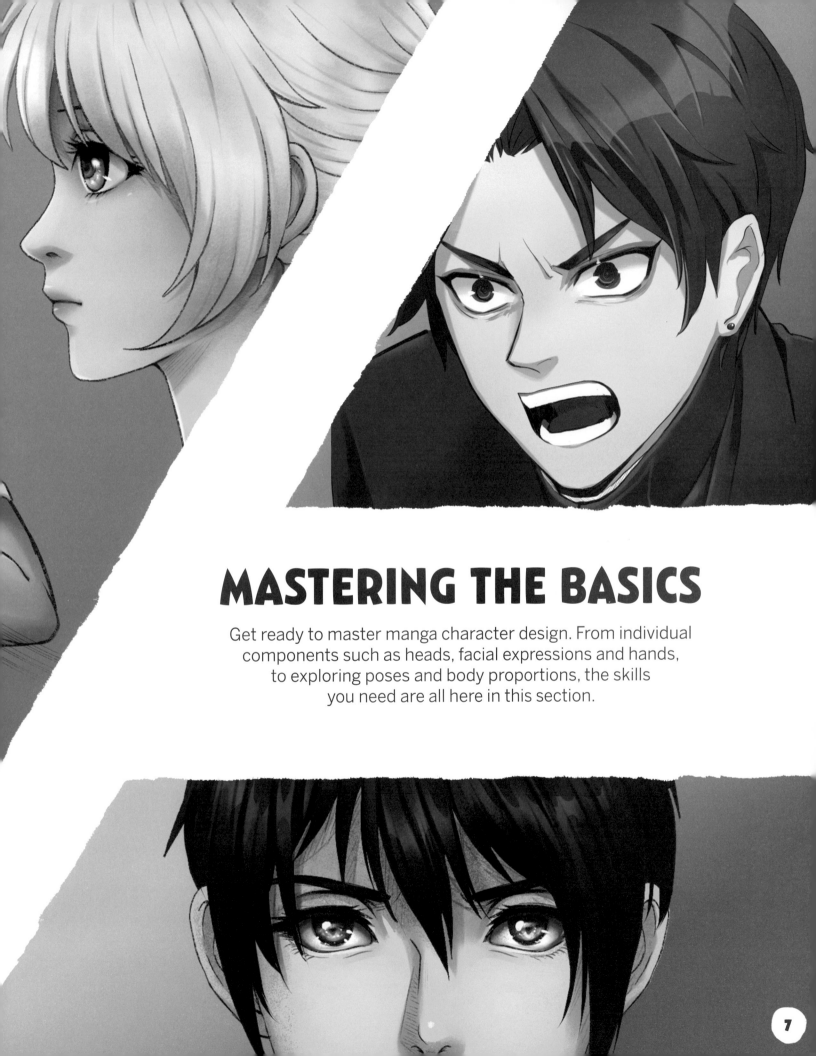

MASTERING THE BASICS

Get ready to master manga character design. From individual components such as heads, facial expressions and hands, to exploring poses and body proportions, the skills you need are all here in this section.

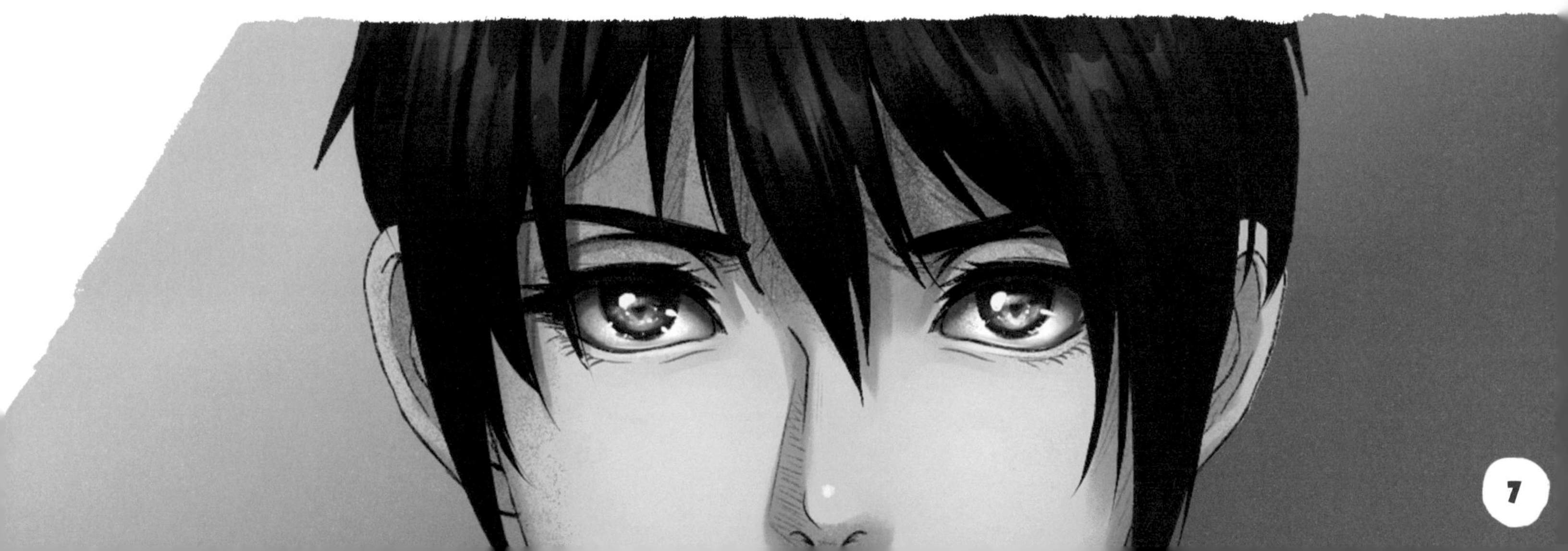

HEADS UP!

The head of any manga character will usually have simple features drawn in clean lines. Get to grips with features, proportions and how to realize different perspectives.

FRONT-ON VIEW

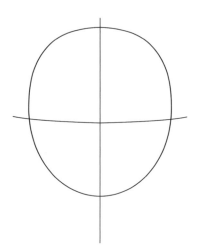

1 For a front-on view, draw a simple oval with guidelines to show the halfway points.

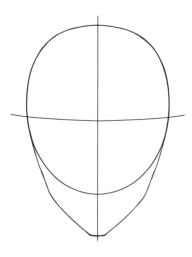

2 A triangular shape added to the bottom of the oval creates the jawline.

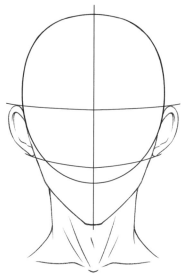

3 Draw a second guideline to help mark the bottom of the ears, as shown. Then, add the ears and neck, too.

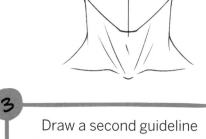

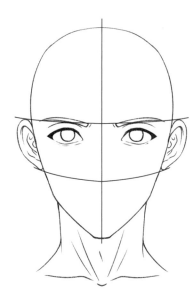

4 Add eyes and eyebrows (see pages 12–13) – the eyelids should align with the top horizontal line. Eye size will vary depending on character.

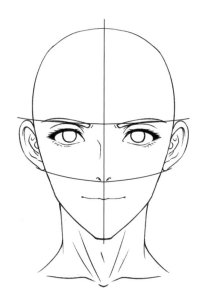

5 The second horizontal line marks the bottom of the nose, and the lips go between the nose and the chin.

6 Once the face is in proportion, sketch some hair for your character (see pages 18–21).

TILTED UP

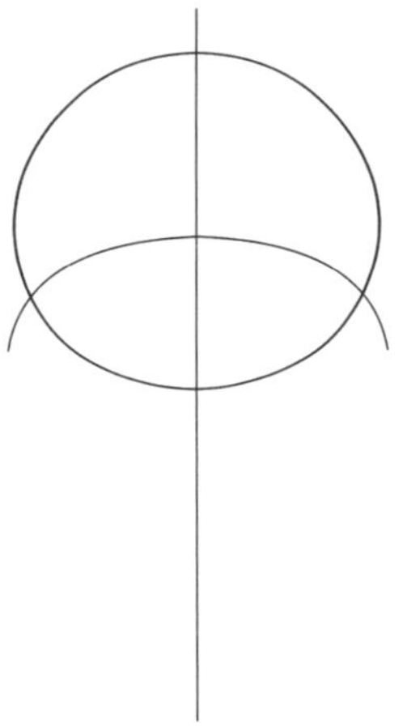

1

For a tilted-up head, start with a squashed circle and central vertical guideline. The second guideline curves downwards.

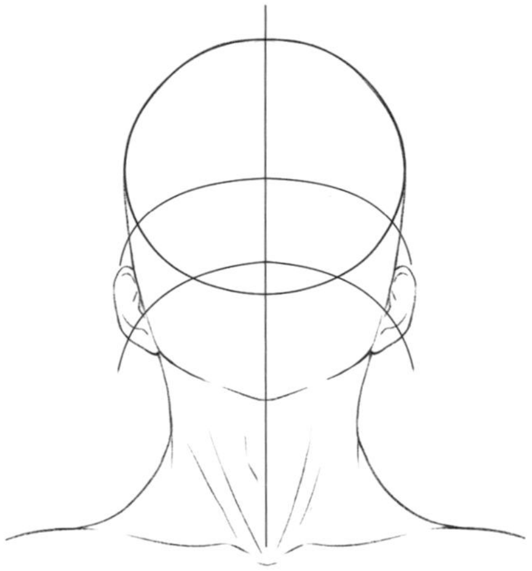

2

Extend the circle downwards to create a jawline. Draw a second curved guideline below the first to mark the lower ears and sketch them in. Add the neck.

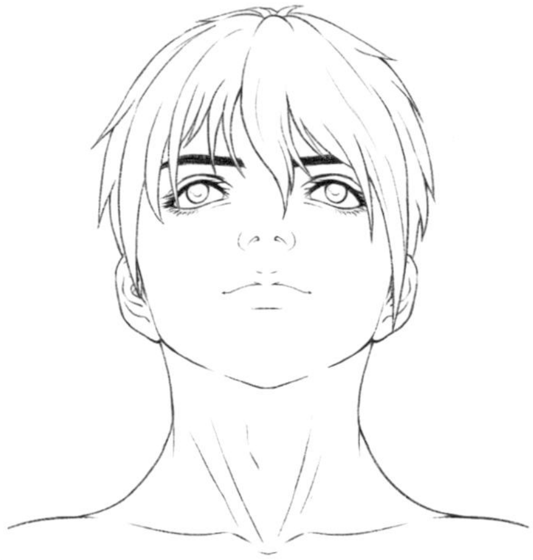

3

Add details to the ears and draw in the remaining facial features. Finally, add the hair.

TILTED DOWN

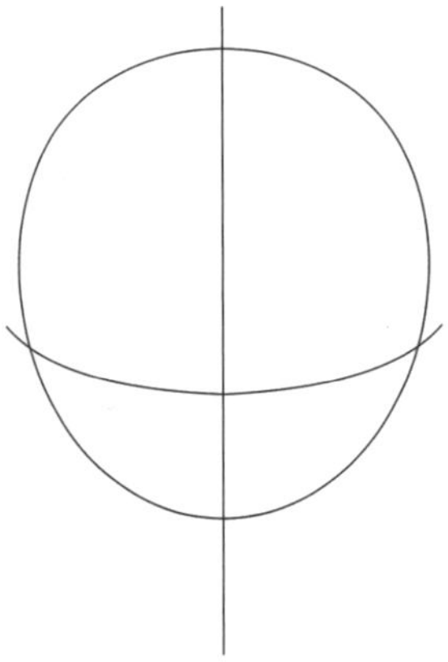

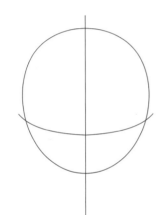

1

For a tilted-down head, draw an oval shape and a vertical guideline. Add a curved guideline two-thirds down the oval, curving upwards.

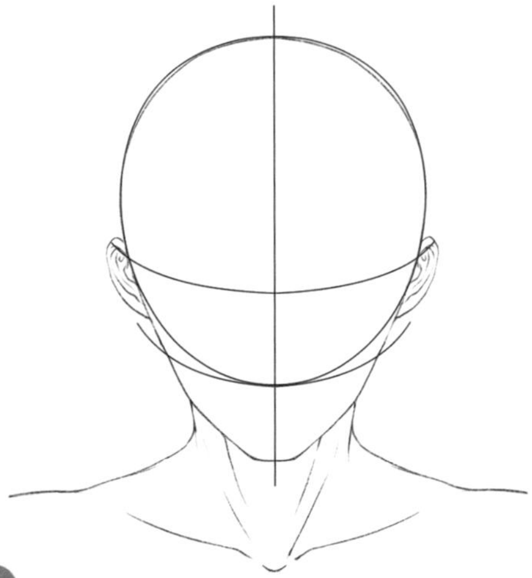

2

Position the ears, with the upper line marking the top of the ears. Draw a narrower jawline and a shorter neck.

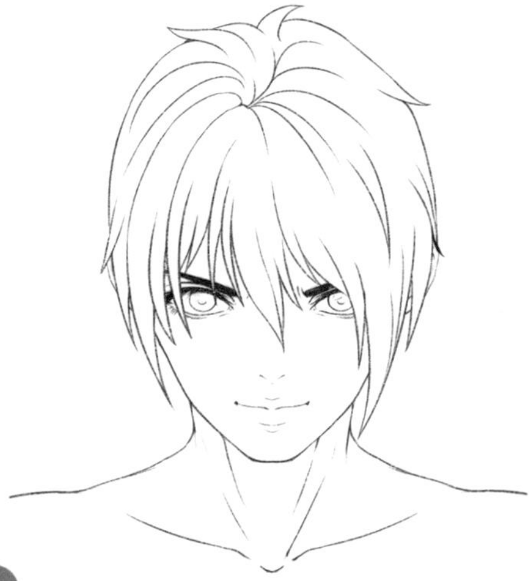

3

Add facial features and hair to finish your character.

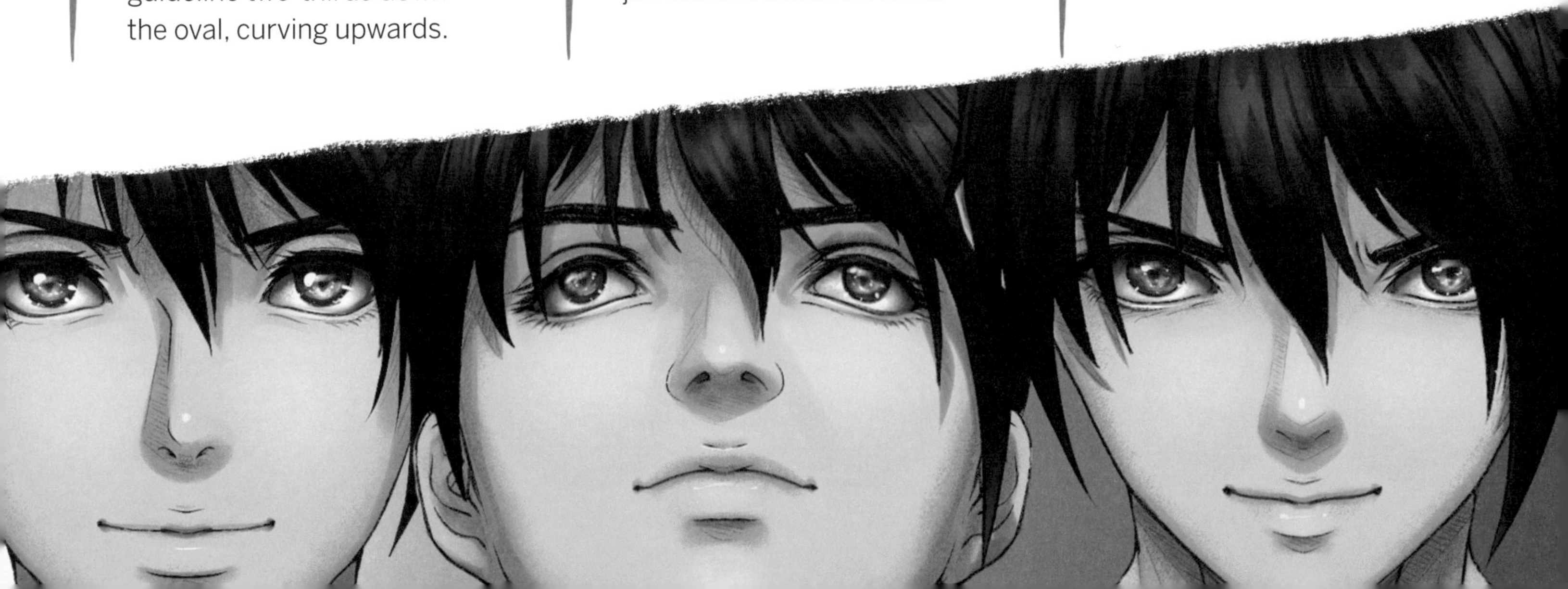

IN PROFILE

In real life, you see people in 3D and from all angles – you want to capture this in manga, too. Learn how to draw side and three-quarter profiles to bring your characters to life.

SIDE PROFILE

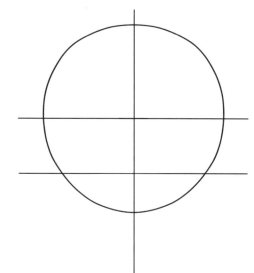

1

Sketch a circle with three guidelines, as shown. The lower horizontal guideline should be halfway between the centre and the bottom of the circle.

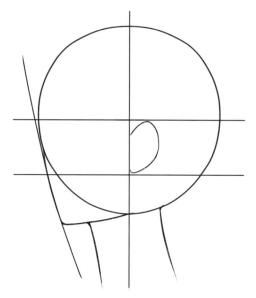

2

Sketch a tilted guideline to mark the front edge of the face. Use it to add a jaw, and position the ear between the horizontal guides. Add the neck.

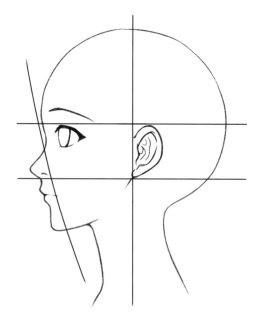

3

The upper horizontal line marks the top line of the eye, and the second marks the bottom of the nose. Unless the hair will be covering the ear, add ear detail, as shown.

4

Sketch in a hairstyle for your character to finish (see pages 18–21).

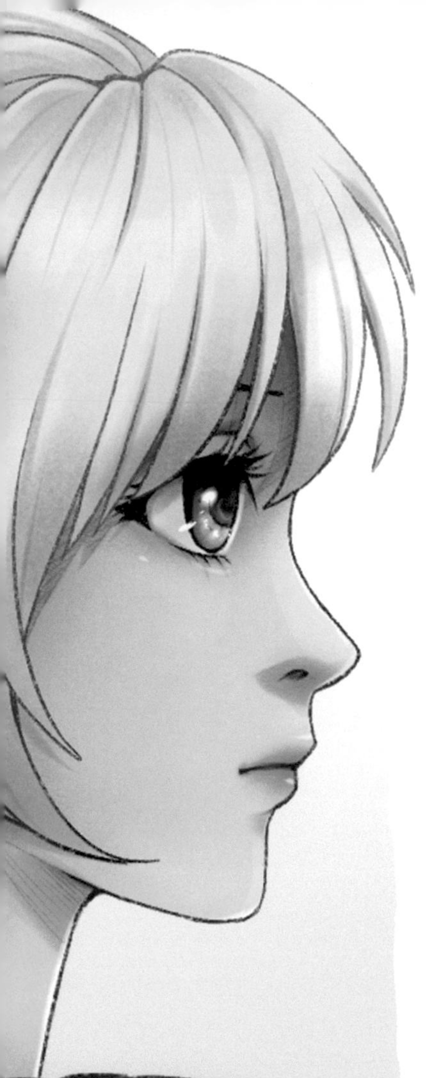

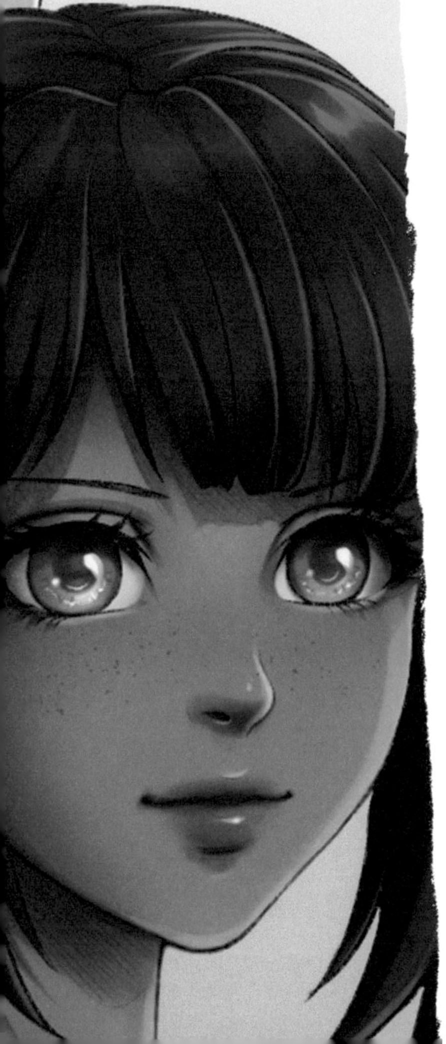

THREE-QUARTER PROFILE

1

A three-quarter profile is halfway between front-on and side profile. Start with a circular shape – this time the guidelines will cross three-quarters to the right.

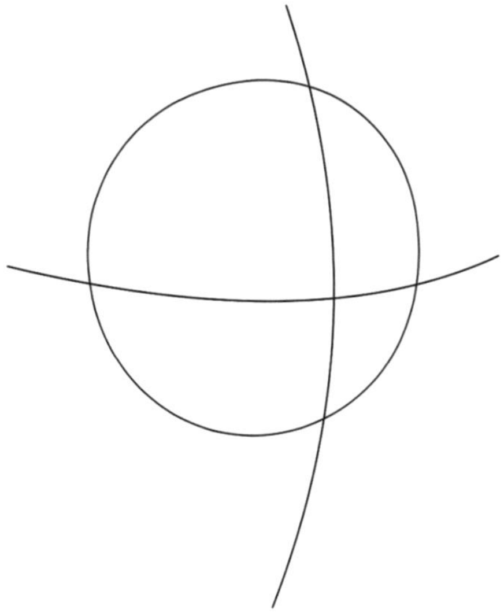

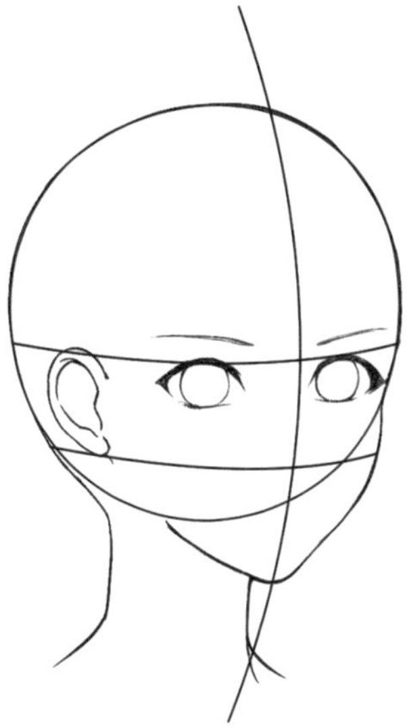

2

Use the guidelines to position the jaw and chin. Add the neck, eyes, eyebrows and ears. The top of the ear should touch the upper horizontal line.

3

Draw the lips, nose and eyelashes, using the guidelines to position them. Notice how the shapes of the features change at different angles.

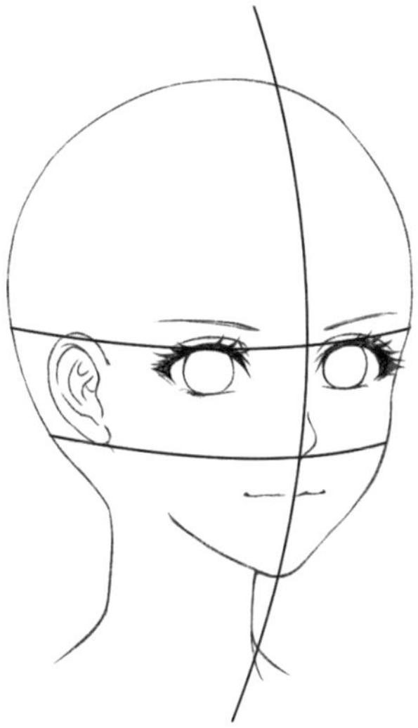

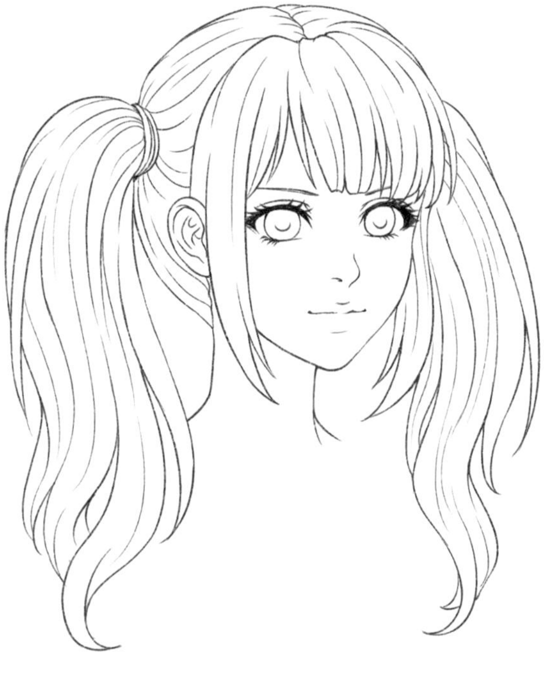

4

Finish the eye detail and add hair. The ear could be visible or hidden behind hair, depending on the hairstyle.

MANGA EYES

Large, expressive eyes are a key feature of manga characters.
While challenging, they can be one of the most fun things to draw, too.

1 Start by drawing two curved guidelines and one central vertical guideline. This will help you position the eyes.

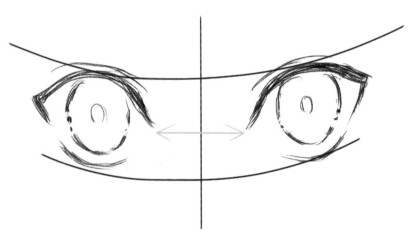

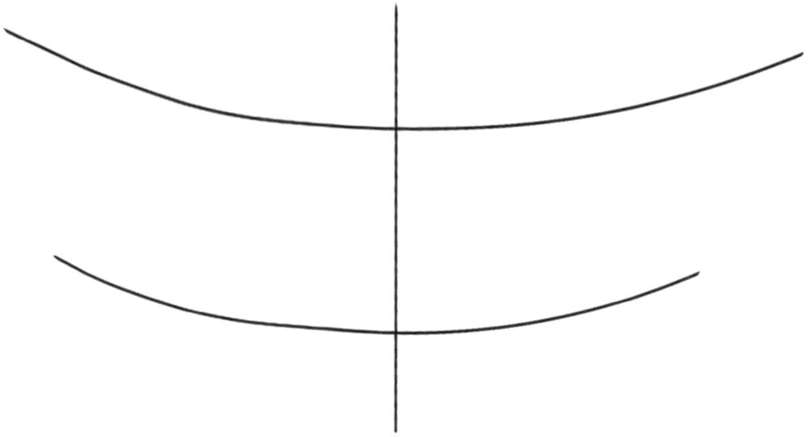

2 Roughly sketch in the eyes and eyelids, fitting them between your guidelines, one eye's width apart.

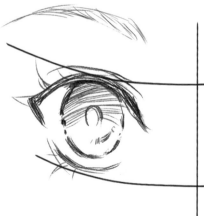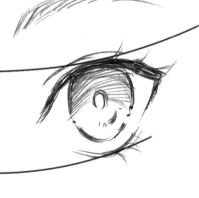

TIP
Adding shading and reflections help bring the eyes to life. It's common in manga for characters to have at least two 'highlights' in the eyes.

3 Add details such as eyelashes and eyebrows. Introduce some shading to the top of the irises.

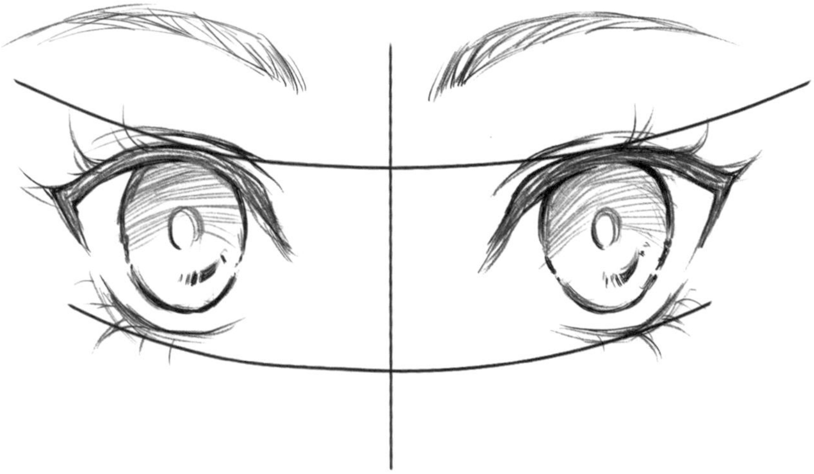

4

Refine your key lines around the eyelids, eyelashes and the outlines of the irises.

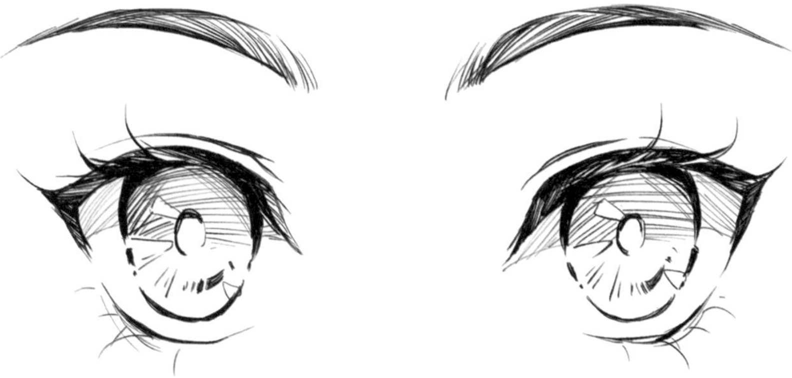

5

Complete the shading. Create the impression of reflections by leaving some white areas within the shading of the irises.

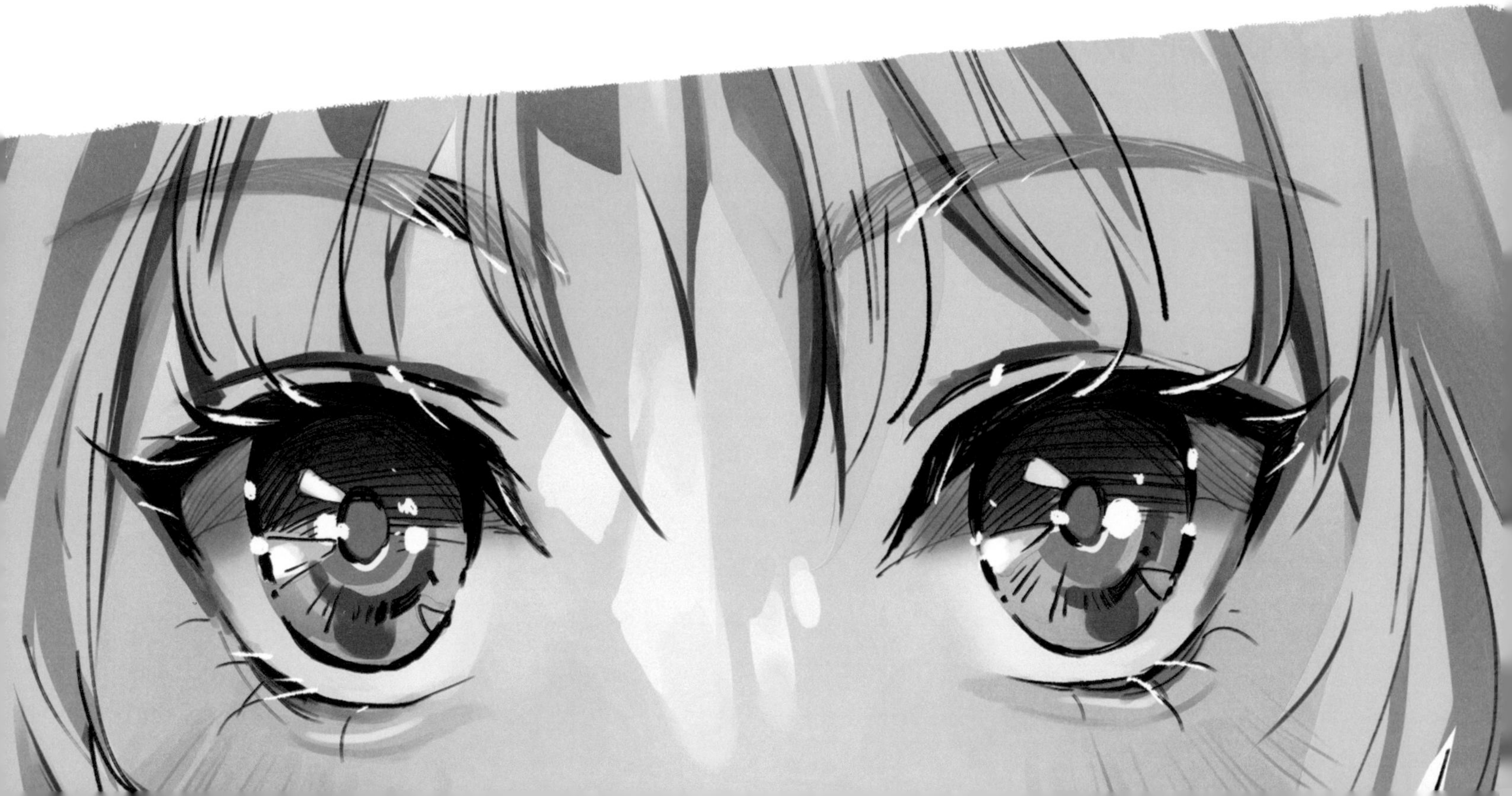

EXPRESSIVE EYES

Once you've mastered the basics, take your manga eyes to the next level. Eyes can be our most expressive physical feature, revealing a wealth of different emotions.

SHOCKED

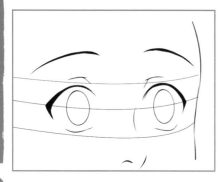

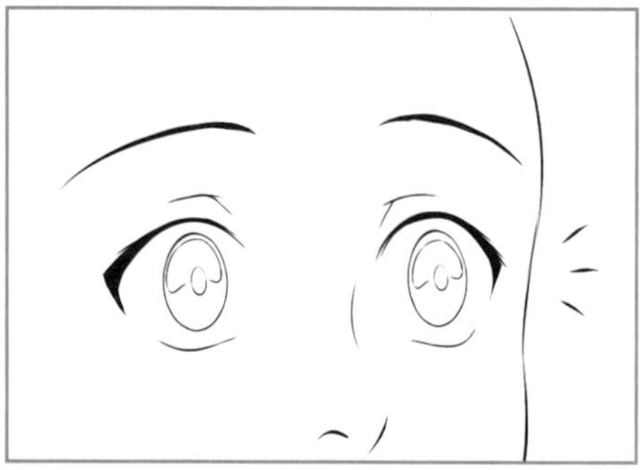

1 Start with your guidelines. To convey shock, make the eyes wide and arch the eyebrows upwards.

2 Leave space around each iris, so more of the whites of the eyes are visible. Add the pupils.

3 Add reflections to give the eyes life. Clean up the lines and refine the details.

EXCITED

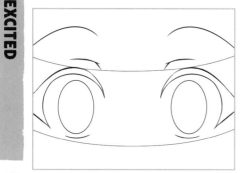

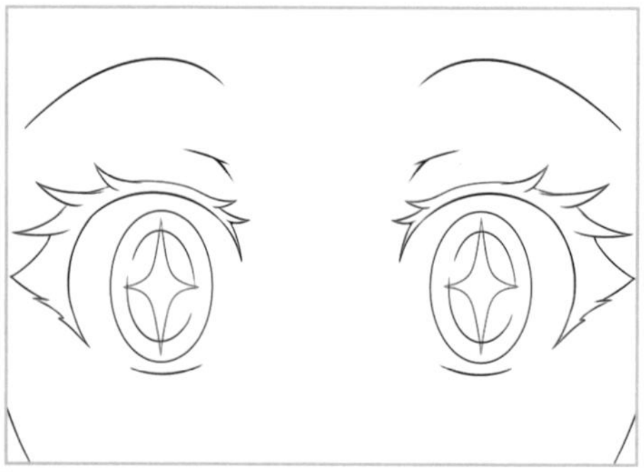

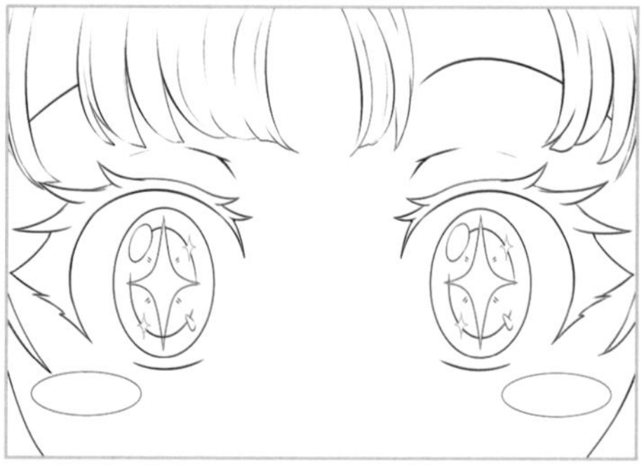

1 Similar to shocked eyes, excited eyes are wide, with eyebrows raised.

2 Add some diamond-shaped sparkles to convey excitement. Sketch the eyelashes.

3 Add more reflections to the eyes. Highlights on the cheeks reveal a slight blush.

DETERMINED

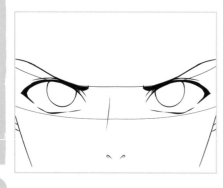

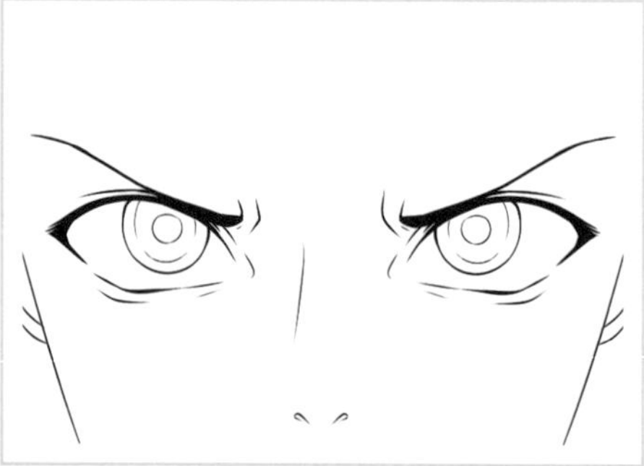

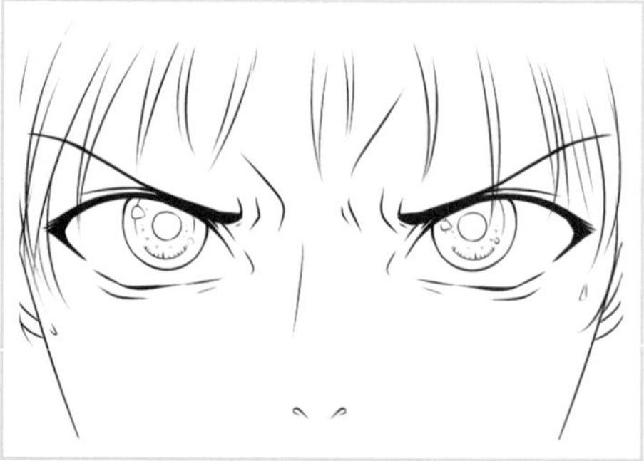

1 The eyes of a determined character are narrow, with low, furrowed eyebrows.

2 Detail the irises and make the pupils small. Wrinkles around the eyes convey concentration.

3 Add further frown lines, shading and small reflections in the eyes to finish.

CYBORG

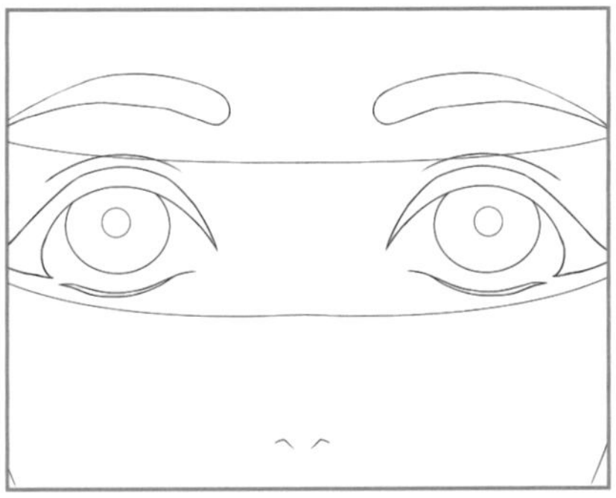

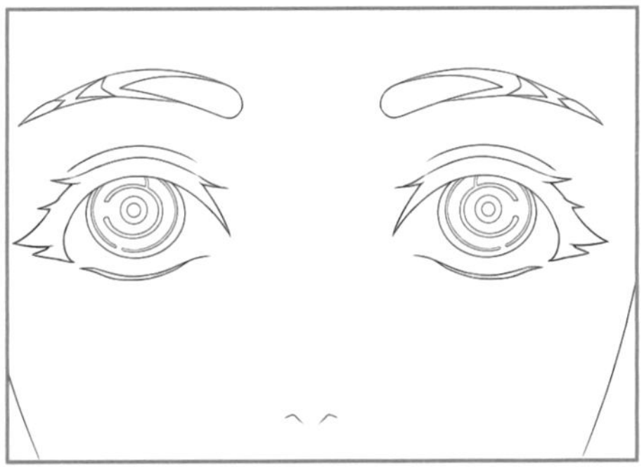

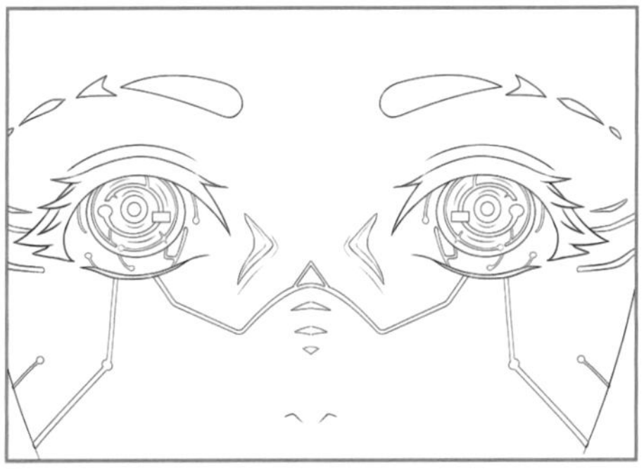

1

This human-mechanical hybrid character has both human and mechanical features.

2

Add concentric circle patterns to the iris, pupils and eyebrows to convey robotic attributes.

3

Further details show where different mechanical parts meet and suggest a metallic texture.

CRYING

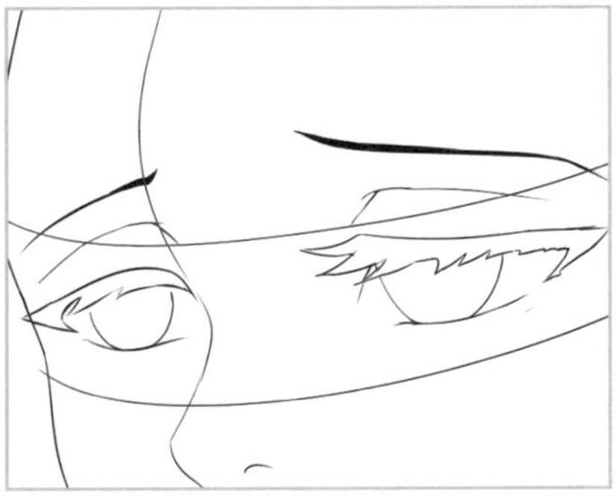

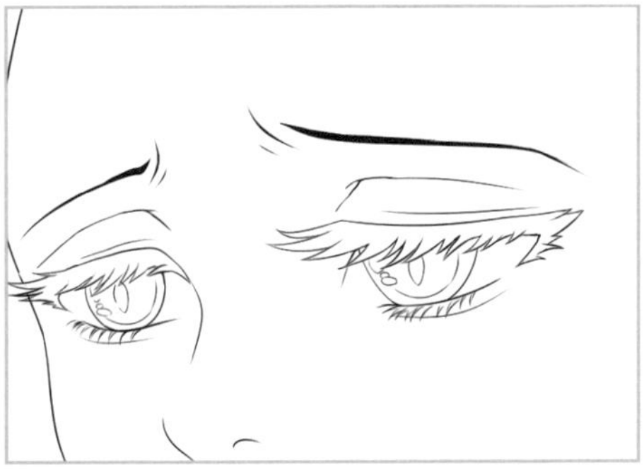

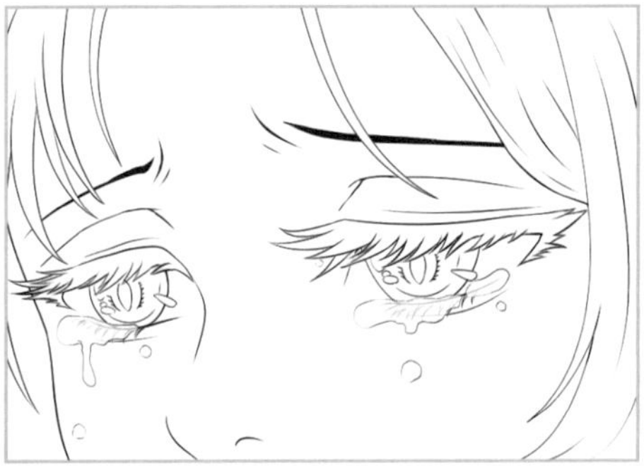

1

With eyes lowered, this character appears upset. Start with a three-quarter profile (see page 11).

2

Add sloping eyebrows and a creased brow. Heavy, downcast eyelashes add to the effect.

3

Outline tears falling over the lower lashes. Make the tears appear 3D by adding reflections.

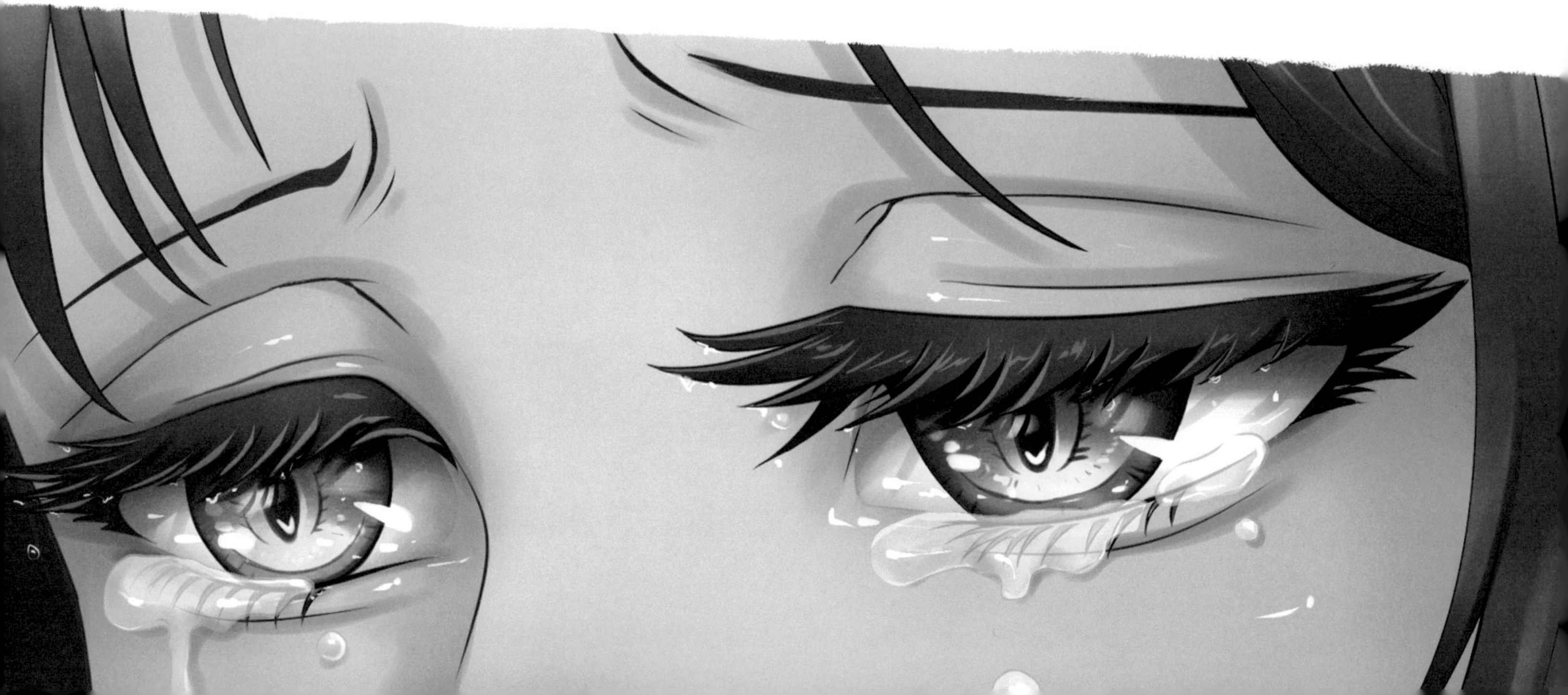

GETTING EMOTIONAL

Emotions bring characters to life. Eyes, eyebrows and mouths are key to conveying anything from joyful happiness to vengeful rage.

JOYFUL

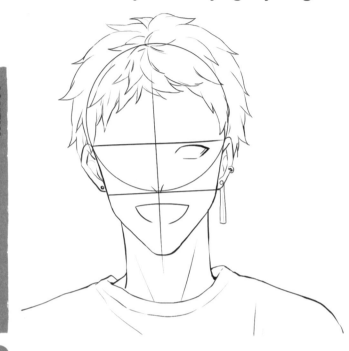

1 Start by drawing guidelines and creating a head, using the techniques you've practised so far.

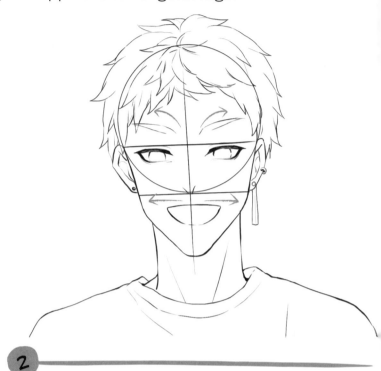

2 When smiling, the eyebrows arch up above the eyes and the mouth stretches outwards.

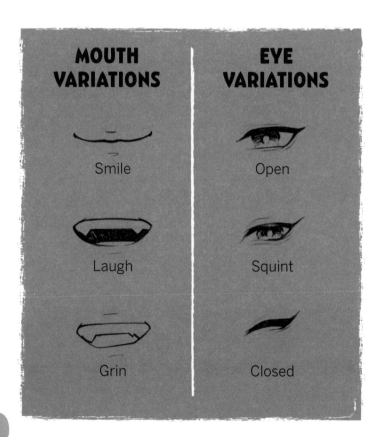

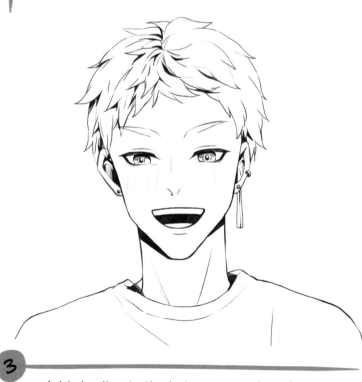

3 Add shading to the hair, ears, neck and eyes, leaving some white areas in the irises.

MOUTH VARIATIONS

Smile

Laugh

Grin

EYE VARIATIONS

Open

Squint

Closed

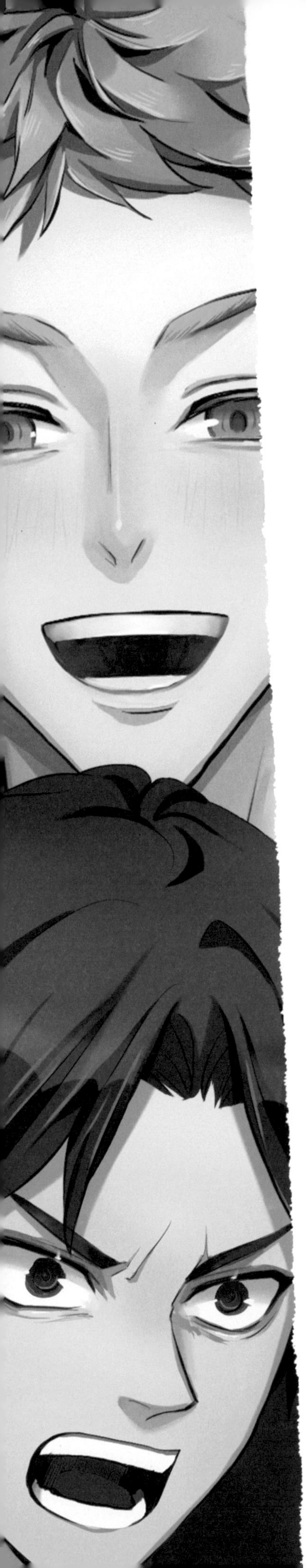

ANGRY

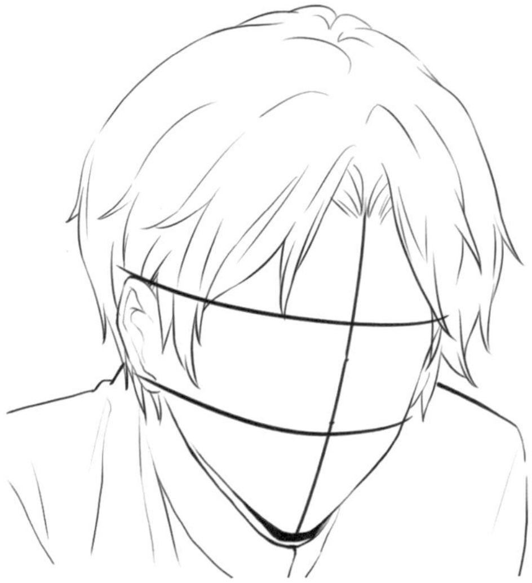

1 To create an angry expression, start with the head and guidelines.

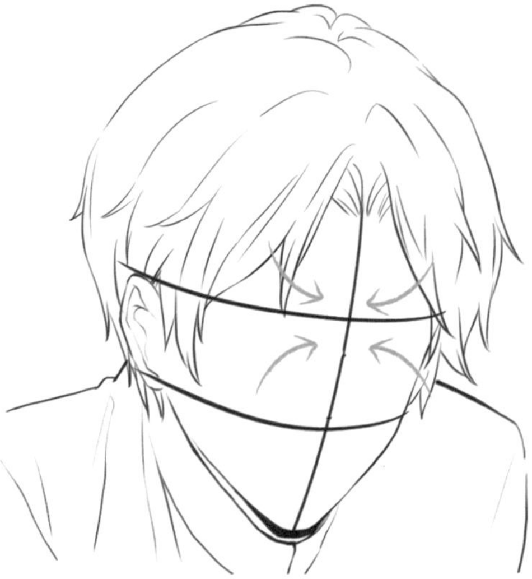

2 Facial features appear to squeeze in when angry.

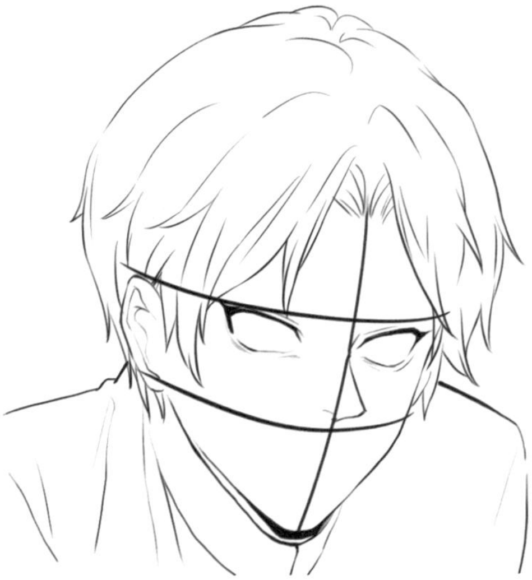

3 Outline the eyes and nose, using the guidelines to position them.

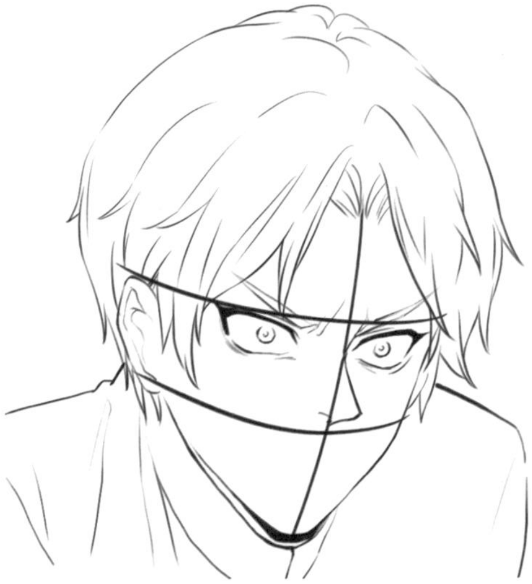

4 Sketch eyebrows in a 'V' shape. The pupils are smaller when angry, which makes the eyes look more intense.

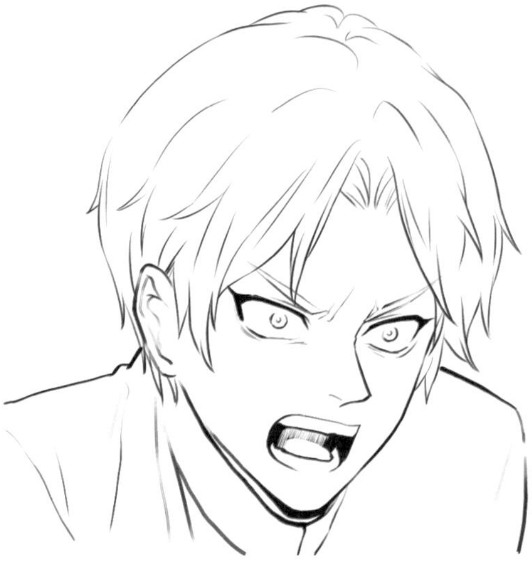

5 Draw the mouth open and narrow, with teeth bared.

NATURAL HAIR

No character is complete without their hair. A hairstyle provides an insight into the personality of a character. How the hair moves can also convey action in an illustration.

1 Define where their hairline falls and mark the crown (the cross) near the back of the head.

2 Strands of hair should 'sprout' away from the head, from the crown.

3 Sketch the hair carefully. Vary the size of the locks for added depth.

4 Add more detail, picking out both thick locks and thinner strands.

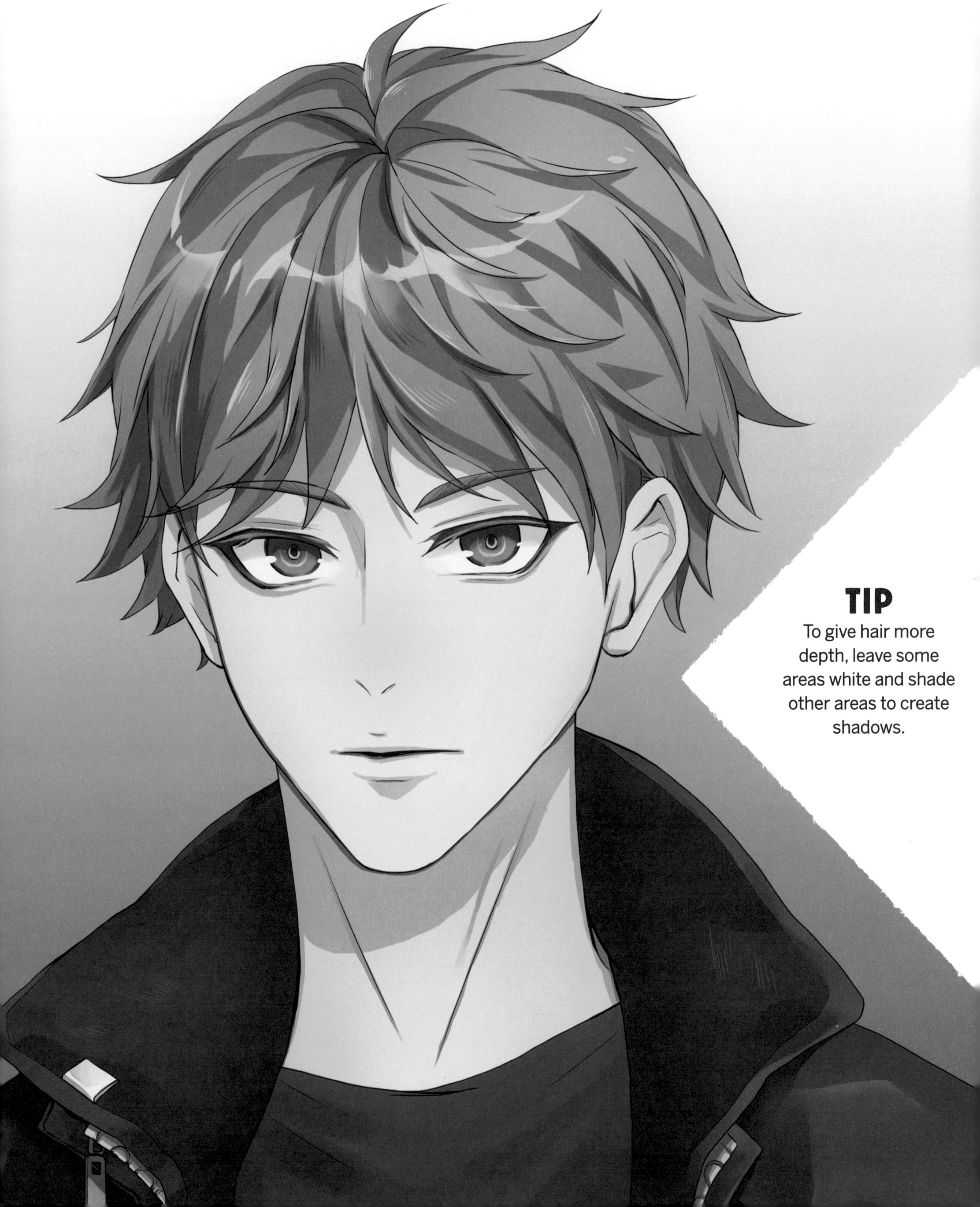

TIP

To give hair more depth, leave some areas white and shade other areas to create shadows.

HAIRSTYLES

This is where you can get really creative, with countless hairstyles to choose from. With each style, think about where on the head the hair is 'sprouting' from and the direction it's flowing in. Texture is also important – is your character's hair smooth or curly?

SPIKY HAIR

1 Start by defining your character's hairline. From the hairline, sketch thick strands of spiky hair flowing away from the face.

2 Continue adding hair across the scalp, following the direction of the hair in front.

PARTING

1 Parted hair falls away from the 'parting', which runs from the hairline to the crown of the head.

2 Your character's parting can be central or to the side – as in this example. Draw hair flowing away from the parting on both sides of the head.

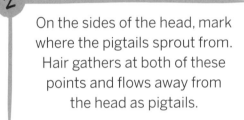

FRINGE AND PIGTAILS

1 ── First sketch the hairline and crown. A fringe will fall forward from the hairline over the face.

2 ── On the sides of the head, mark where the pigtails sprout from. Hair gathers at both of these points and flows away from the head as pigtails.

FRINGE AND BOB

1 ── For a short hairstyle with a fringe, start with the hairline and crown. Mark where the fringe will fall from – either on the hairline or further back towards the crown.

2 ── Draw the fringe falling forward, as before. The rest of the hair will fall away from the crown and the parting on either side of the head.

DRAWING HANDS

Hands can be one of the more intimidating parts of the body to draw.
Get to grips with the underlying structure to make drawing them feel easier.

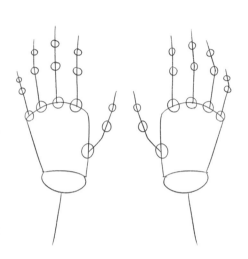 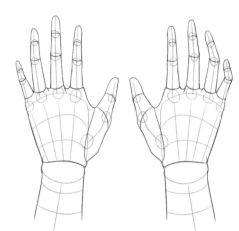 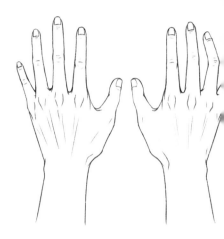

1 Use basic shapes and lines to create a hand, wrist and fingers. Use small circles to represent joints and knuckles.

2 Flesh out your guidelines; fingers should only bend at the joints. Notice how the knuckles (above) and palm (below) create contours.

3 When the palm is down (above), draw the tendons converging at the wrist. When the hand faces up (below), include palm lines.

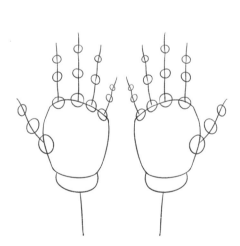  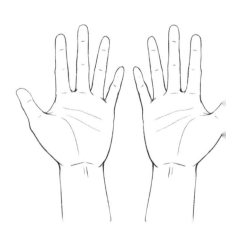

Follow the three-step process on page 22 to try out a range of different hand gestures.

FIST

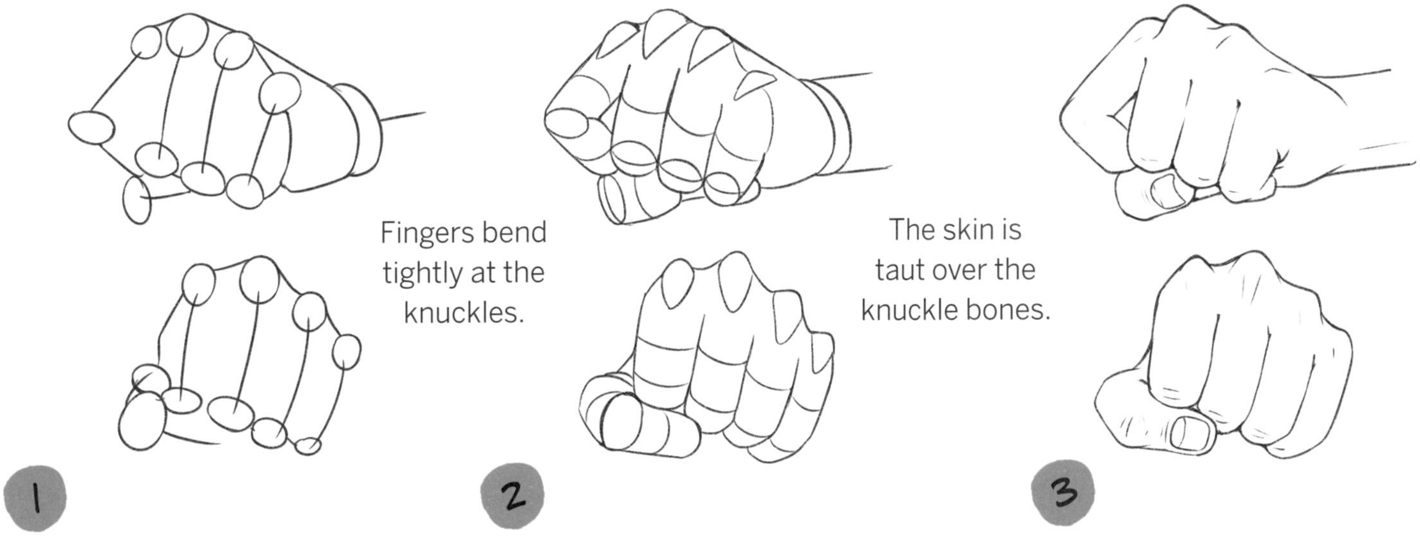

Fingers bend tightly at the knuckles.

The skin is taut over the knuckle bones.

FINGER PRESS

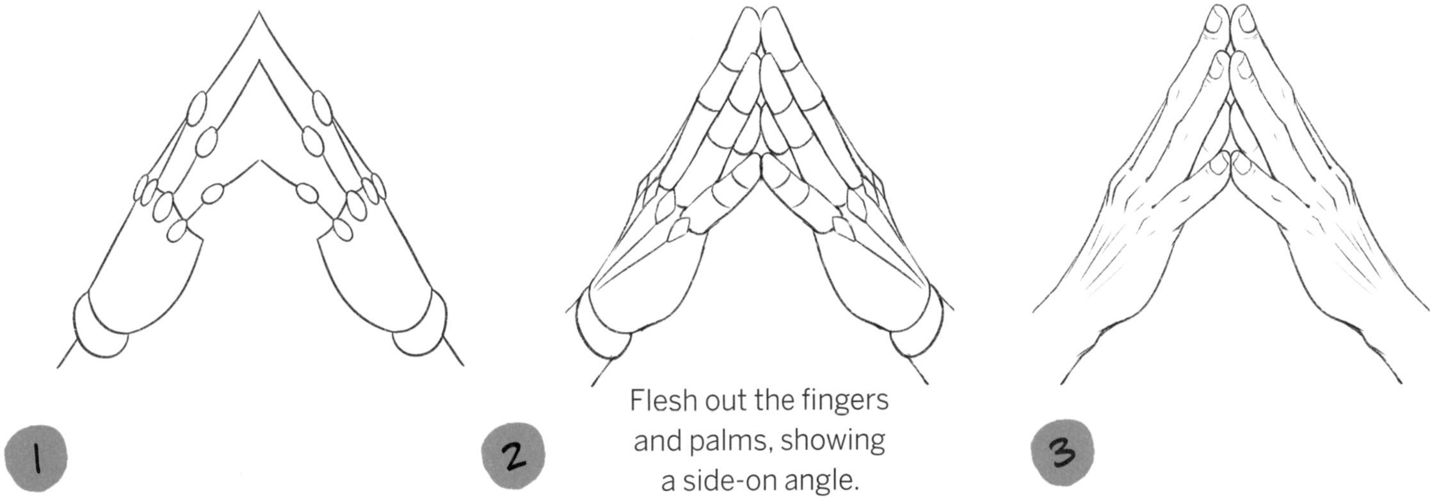

Flesh out the fingers and palms, showing a side-on angle.

THUMBS UP

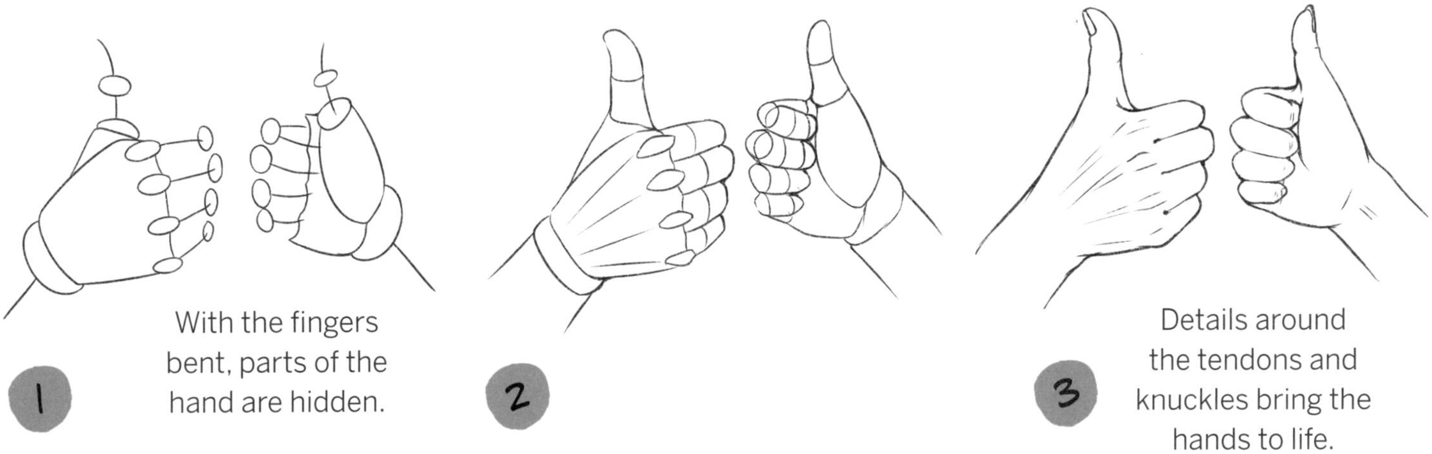

With the fingers bent, parts of the hand are hidden.

Details around the tendons and knuckles bring the hands to life.

UPRIGHT STANDING POSE

Learn this technique to make sure your characters' bodies are in proportion. In manga, this is called 'toushin' (pronounced 'toe-shin'), and refers to the head to body ratio.

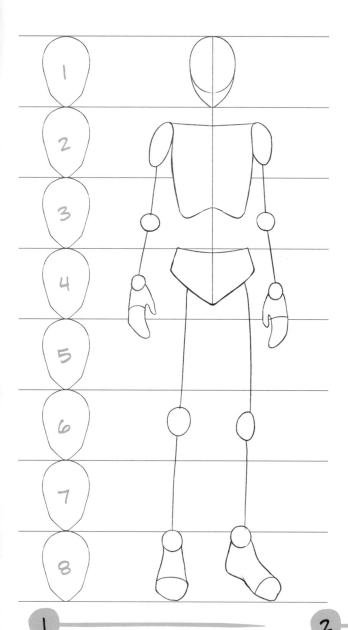

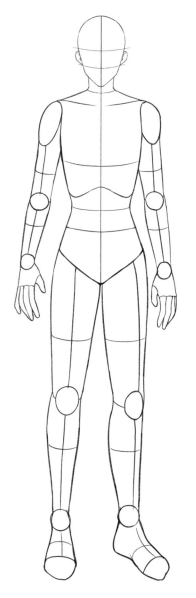

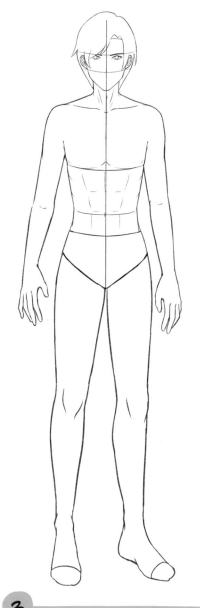

1 Sketch the head and use it as a guide for the height of your character: eight heads tall is average. Create the frame of the body, made up of key joints and bones, in the proportions shown.

2 Flesh out the frame you have created. Don't worry about details yet – look closely at proportions.

3 Next, add details to the body. Sketch the pectoral muscles at roughly two heads down and the belly button at three heads down.

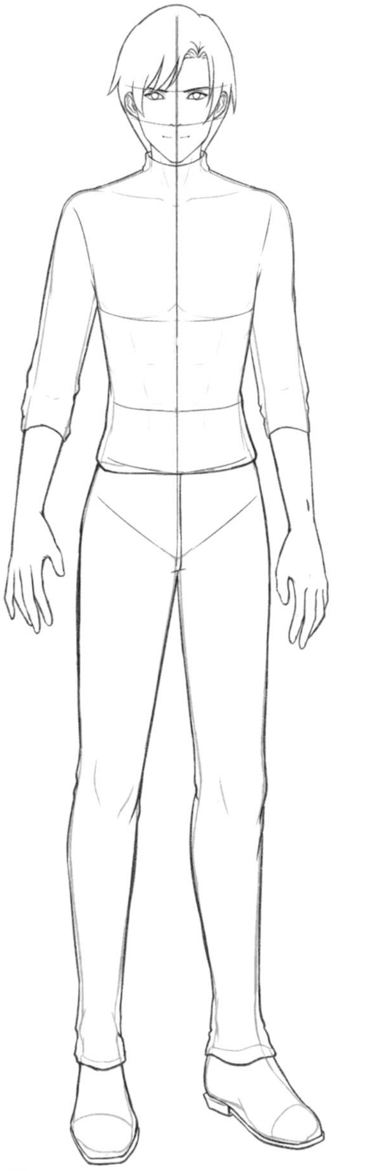

4

Complete the facial features and hair. Sketch clothes over the body.

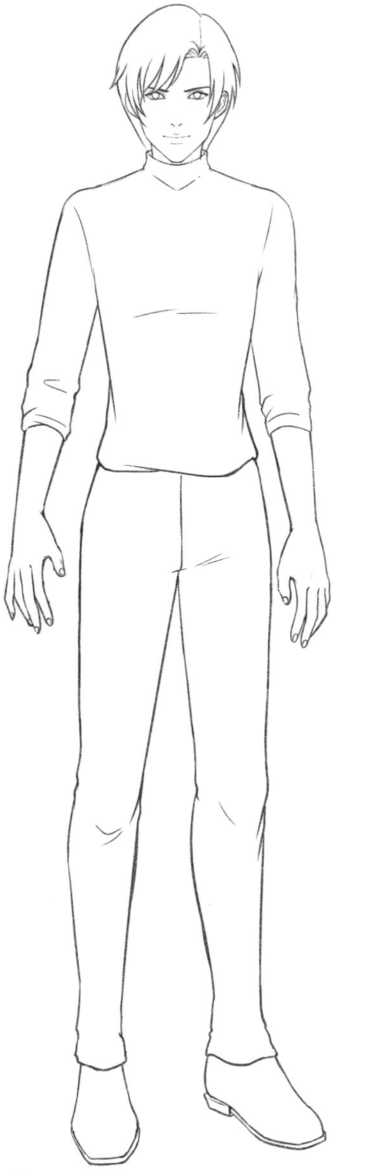

5

Add creases in areas where the material wrinkles, for example, at the elbows and knees.

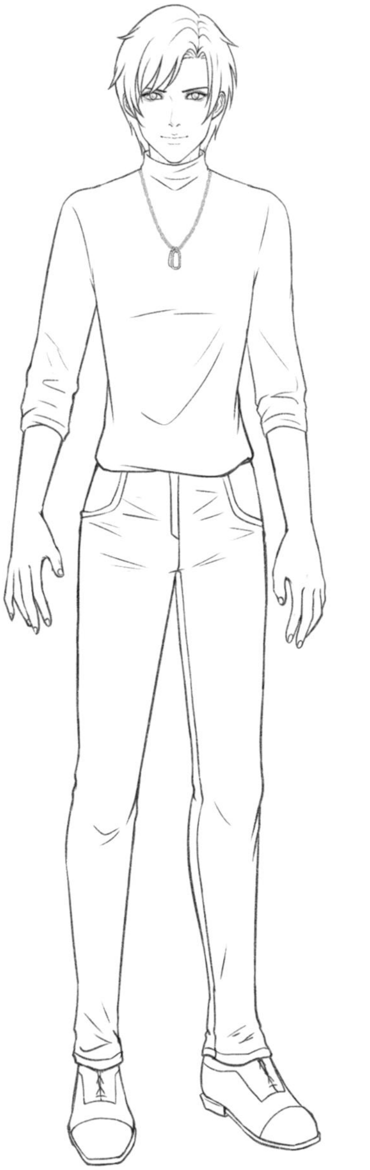

6

Finish your character by adding accessories and any extra details.

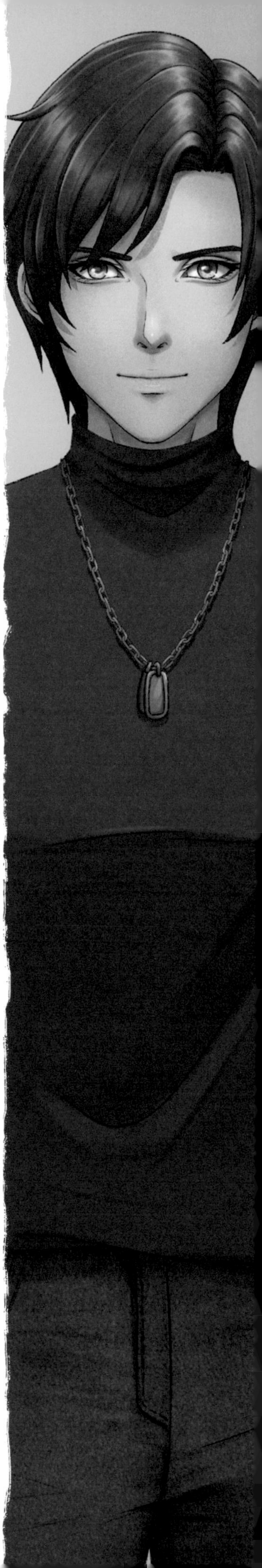

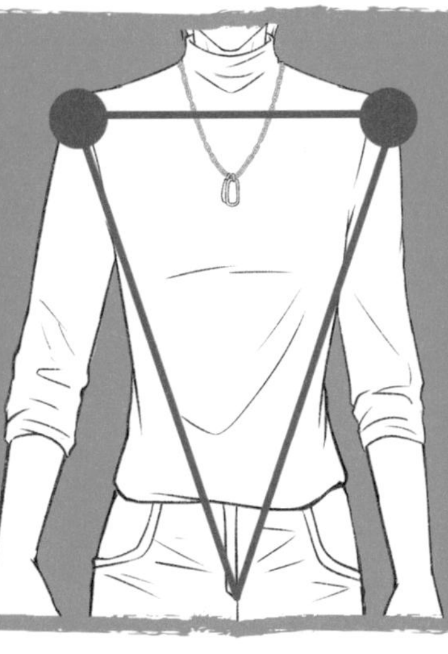

EXTRA DETAIL

Generally, male characters have broader shoulders than hips – you can use a triangle to check your proportions.

The shoulders and hips of female characters are roughly equal widths – use two triangles to check your proportions.

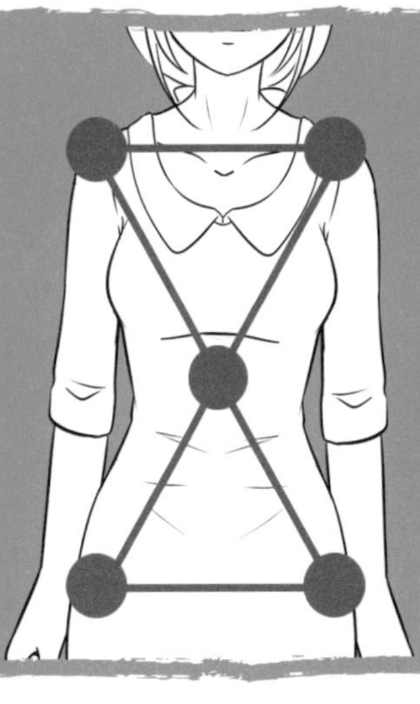

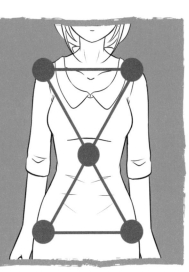

RELAXED STANDING POSE

No manga character can be in the thick of the action all the time. Master a relaxed, casual pose for when your characters are feeling more chilled.

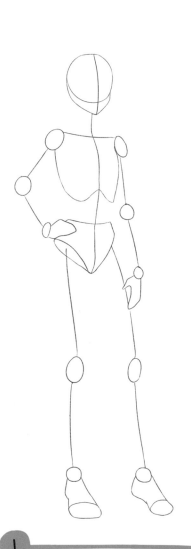

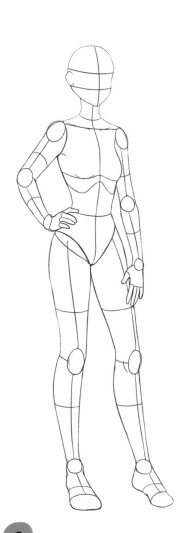

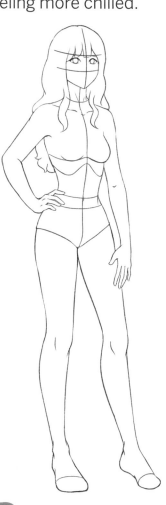

1 Sketch the head and use it as a guide to draw the frame. Create a skeletal structure that highlights joints, such as knees, elbows and shoulders.

2 Flesh out the frame. The body's weight falls more on the leg on the left, and so the central line of the body goes down through this leg.

3 Add body details to the torso, waist and knees. Draw in the fingers and outline the hair and eyes.

EXTRA DETAIL
Fingers and hands can be fiddly. Start with simple shapes, before adding fingers, knuckles and fingernails (see pages 22–23).

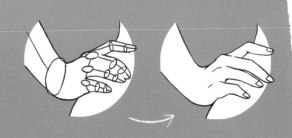

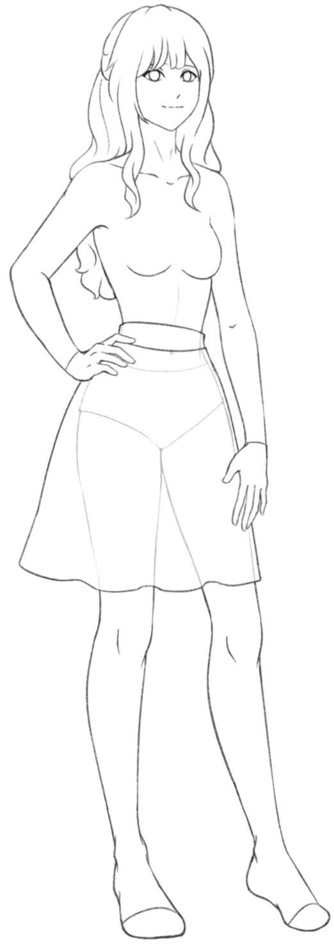

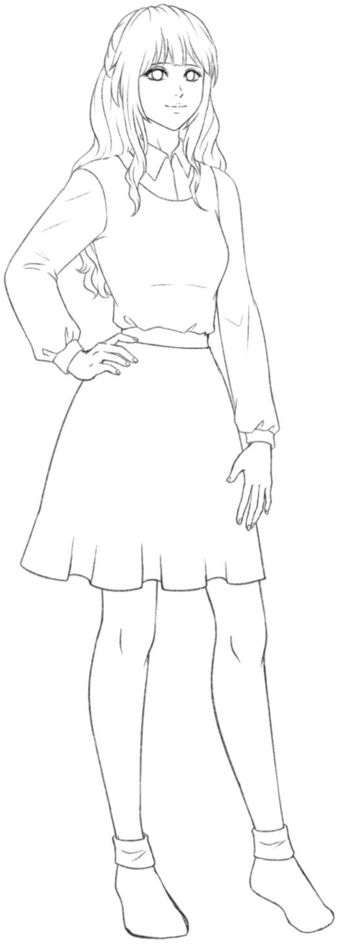

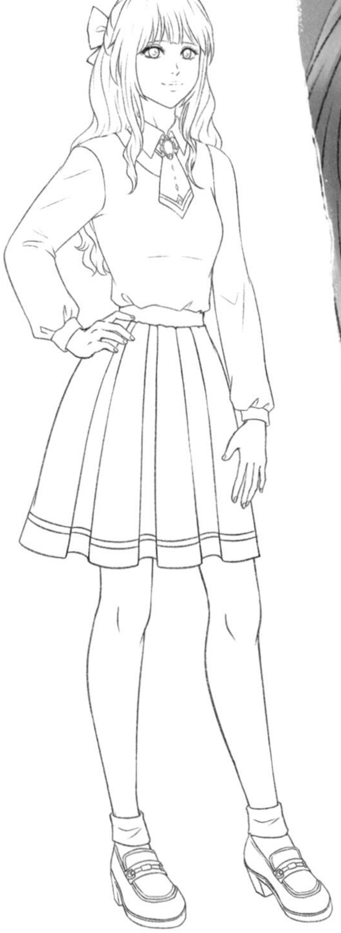

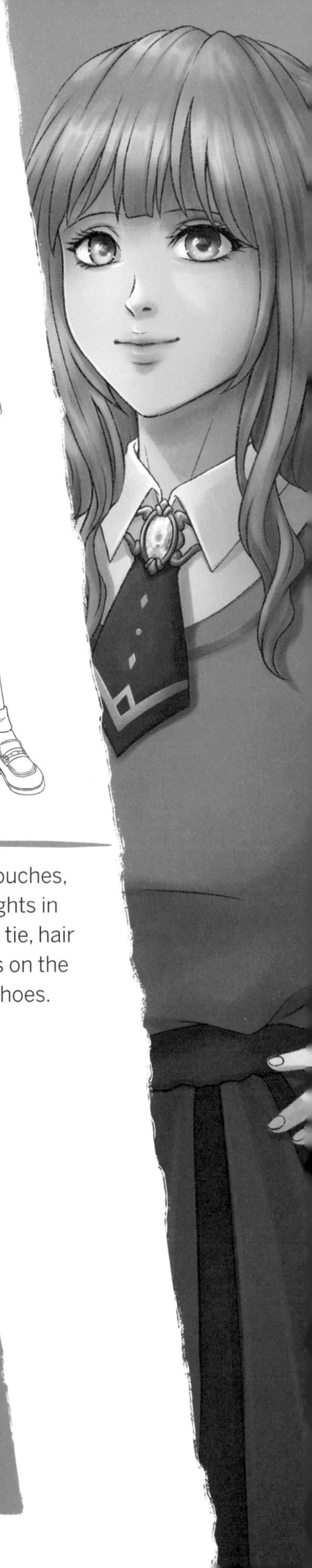

4

Start to develop the skirt, hair and facial features, matching the angle of the face (see page 11).

5

Design your character's outfit, noting where the creases of the clothes fall due to the body's form.

6

Add finishing touches, such as highlights in the eyes, a neck tie, hair bow and details on the clothes and shoes.

EXTRA DETAIL

The arch of the foot will change, depending on the height of the heel. A higher heel calls for a higher arch. Beware – a completely flat arch will look unnatural.

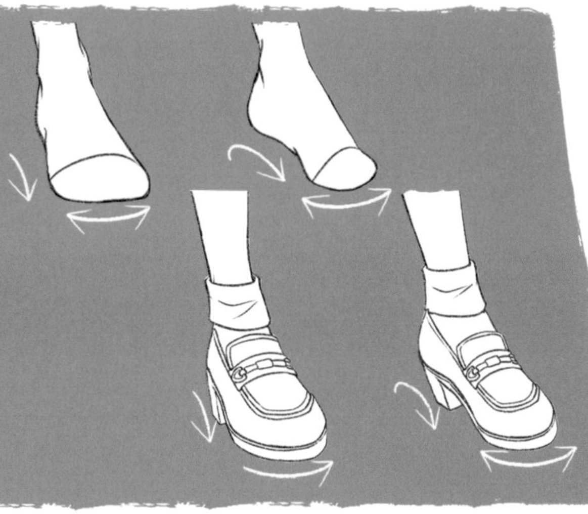

ACTION POSES

This cool three-point landing pose is characterized by a character dropping from up high and landing with their feet apart and body supported by one arm.

THREE-POINT LANDING

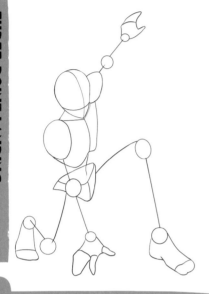

1 Start with the skeletal structure. Notice how the back leg and arm are angled backwards and therefore foreshortened (look shorter).

2 Flesh out the character and their build. The weight of the figure falls on the feet and front hand, creating balance.

3 Begin adding details such as muscles and facial features. Draw hair flying upwards to show that they've just landed.

4 Complete the face and outline the clothes. They may need some heavyweight boots for this kind of landing.

5 Add extra details, such as harnesses, buckles and gloves to give your character style.

6 Refine the facial details and hair. Add motion blur – sharp, upward-pointing strokes – for extra drama (see page 59).

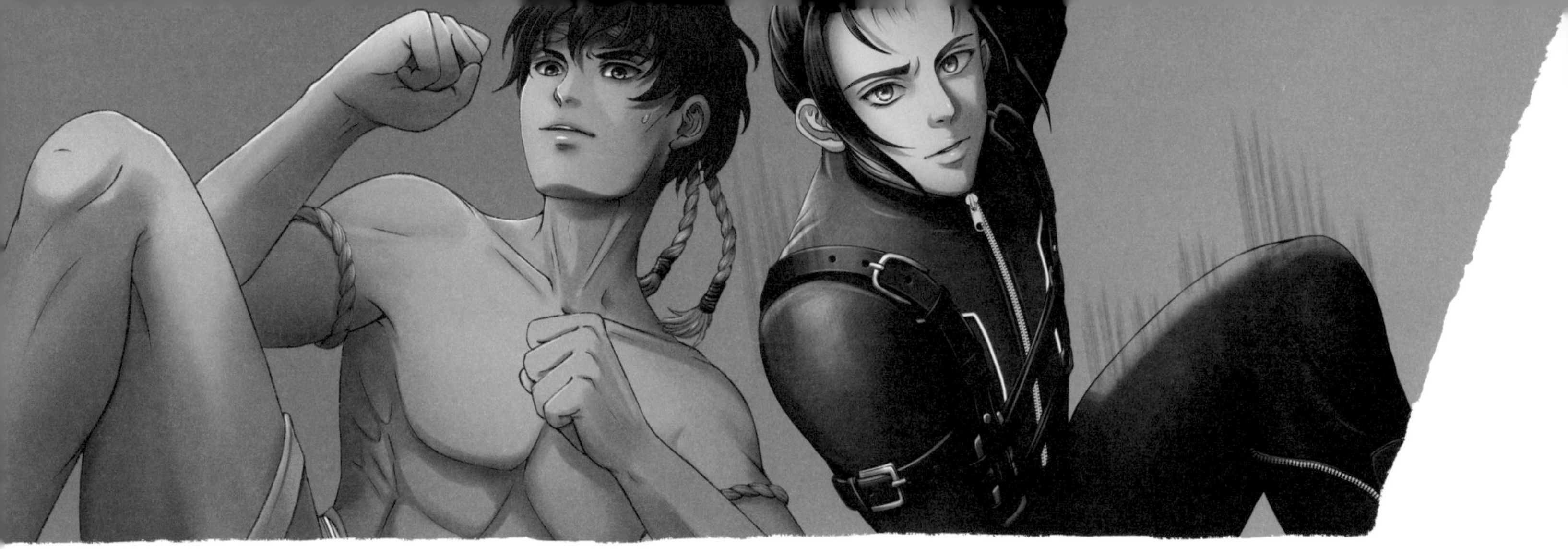

KICK-BOXING POSE

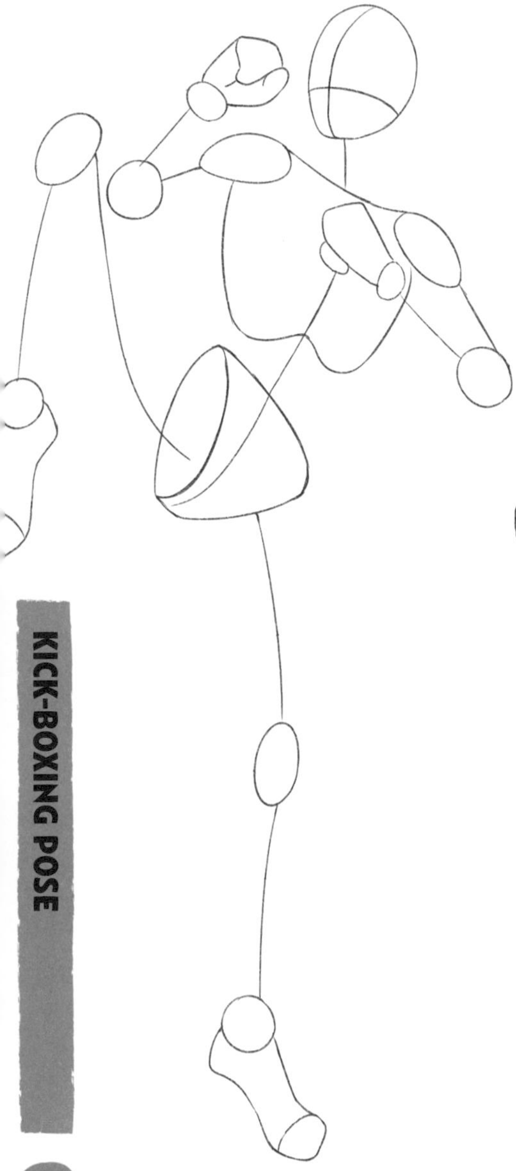

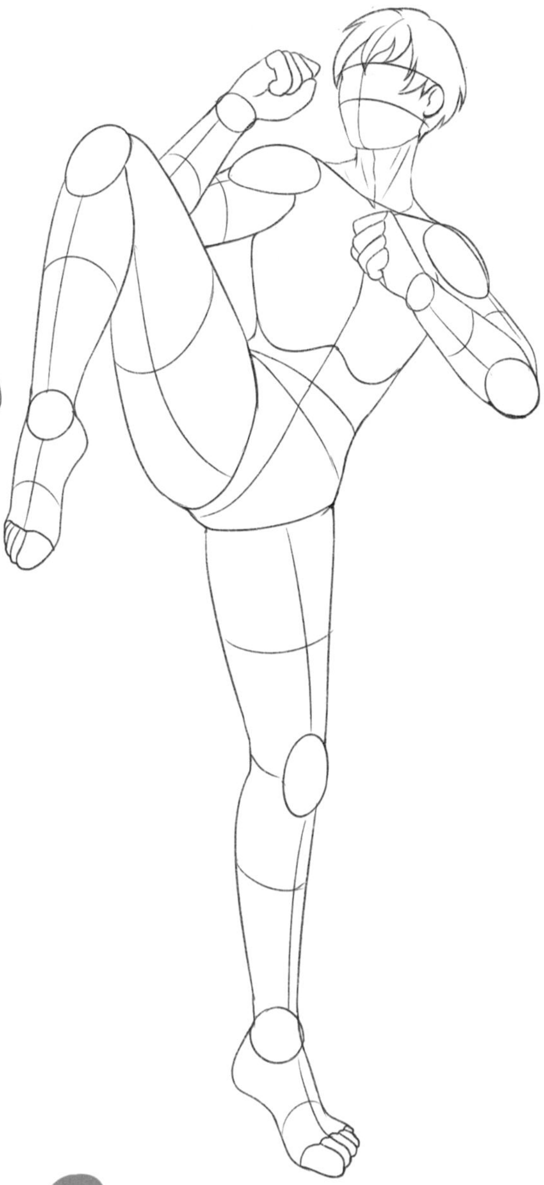

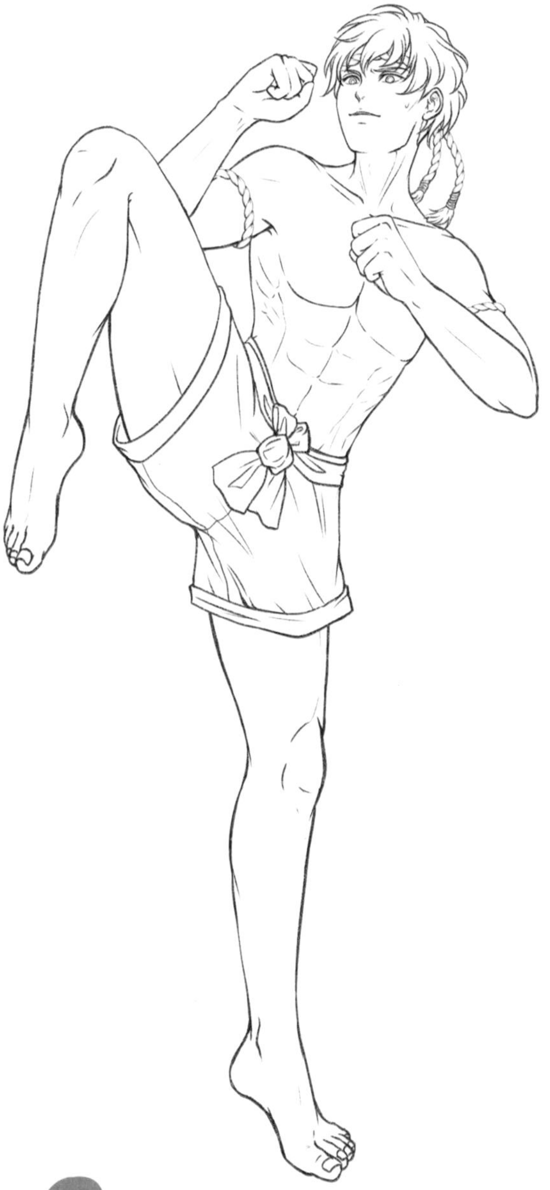

1

For a dynamic kick-boxing pose, start with the basic skeletal structure. Pay attention to the extreme angles of the limbs.

2

Sketch the guidelines and flesh out the build. The weight falls on one leg and the arms are lifted for balance and readiness.

3

Add muscles, clothes, hair and facial details to complete your character.

ON THE RUN

There's a lot going on in a running pose, from the foreshortening of limbs and twisting of the body as muscles tense up, to creating a sense of balance while on the move.

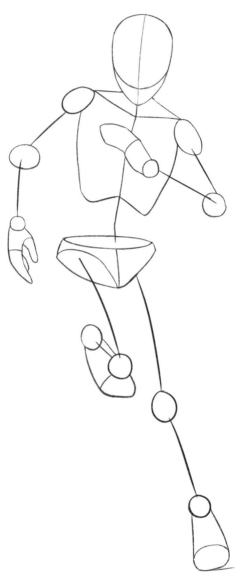

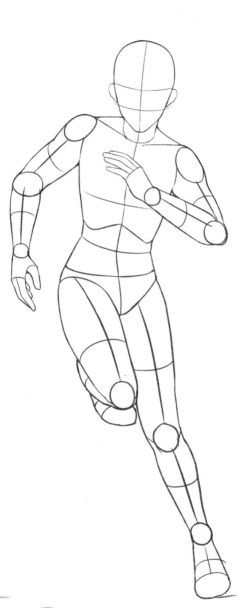

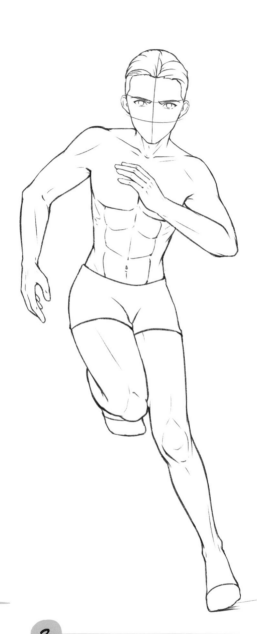

1 Start by sketching the skeletal frame, paying attention to where the joints go.

2 When building the form, work out which leg will be in front. The leg that is forward will usually appear a little larger.

3 Outline the hair and eyes, and use your guidelines to sketch muscles. Understanding the body's form will help when drawing clothing.

TIP
When the right leg moves forward, so does the left arm, and vice versa.

EXTRA DETAIL

Notice how the shoulders and hips tilt in opposite directions here, creating a balanced posture, as the muscles compress on one side.

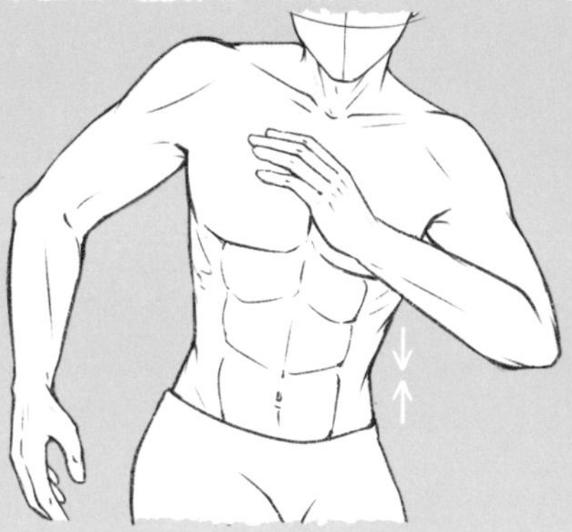

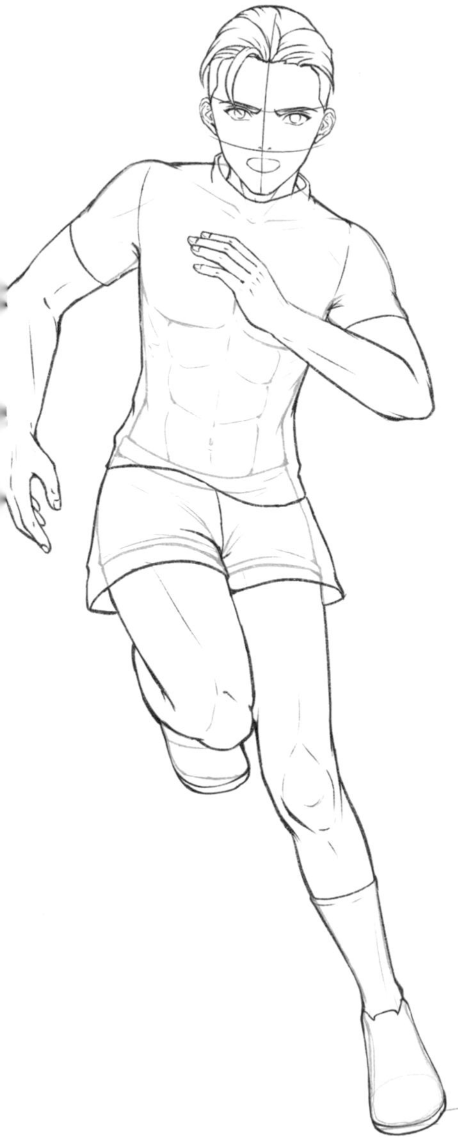

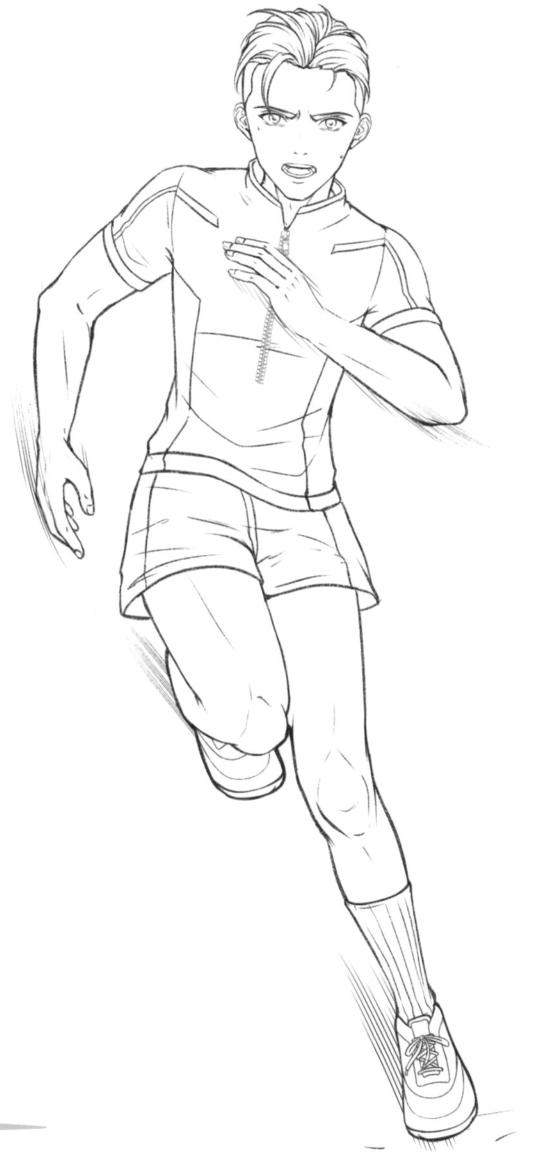

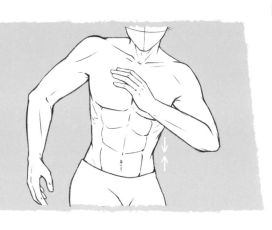

4

Develop the facial features and hair. Sketch clothes and shoes, paying attention to where creases will fall.

5

Finish the final details – a few beads of sweat add to the dramatic effect! Add motion blur around the limbs to convey movement.

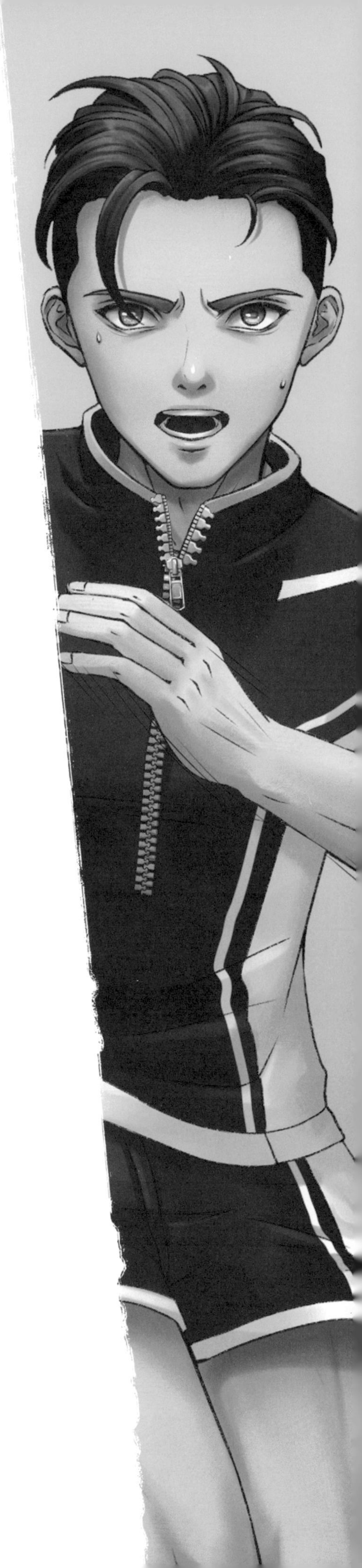

PLAYFUL JUMPING POSE

Next up, create a fun, jumping character making 'V' signs. For an excited pose, try making the eyes wide and eyebrows arched, and add a bouncy hairstyle.

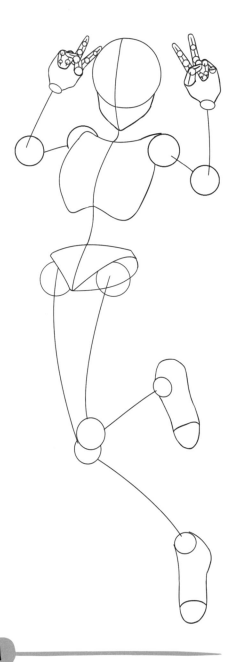

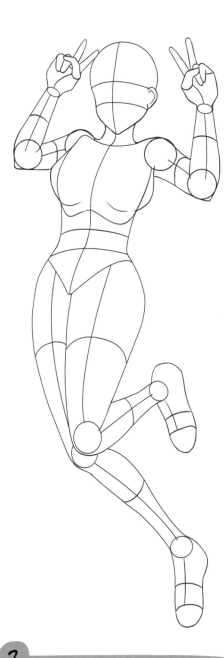

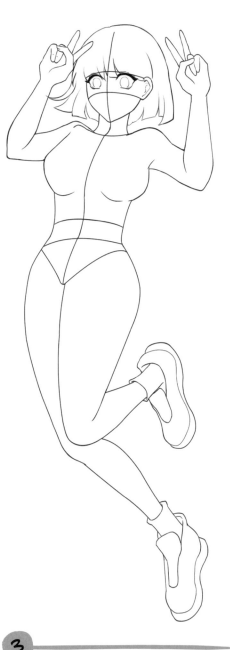

1 Start by plotting the skeletal structure and joints, with arms bent and hands held either side of the face. As the character is jumping, both feet are raised off the floor.

2 Curved guidelines determine the 3D shape of the body as you flesh it out. Facial guidelines curve downwards due to the upwards tilt of the head.

3 Draw in expressive eyes, a fun hairstyle and outline the shoes. Hair flicks upwards, suggesting movement.

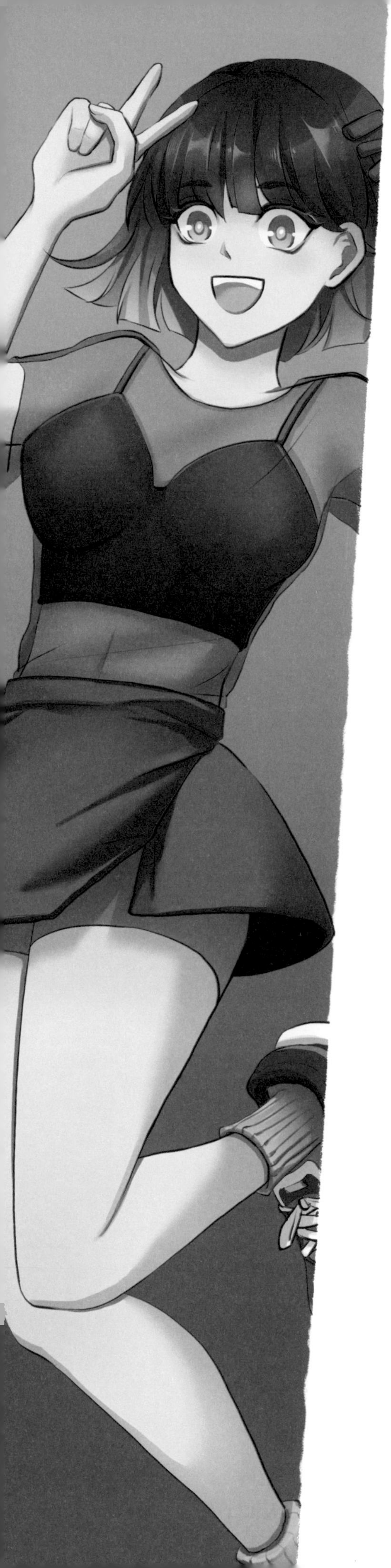

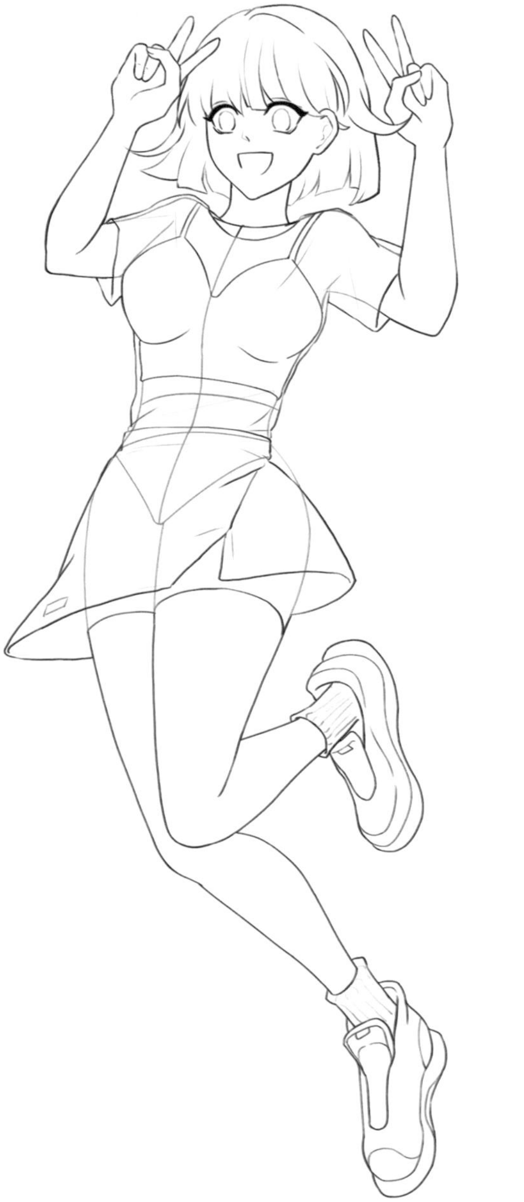

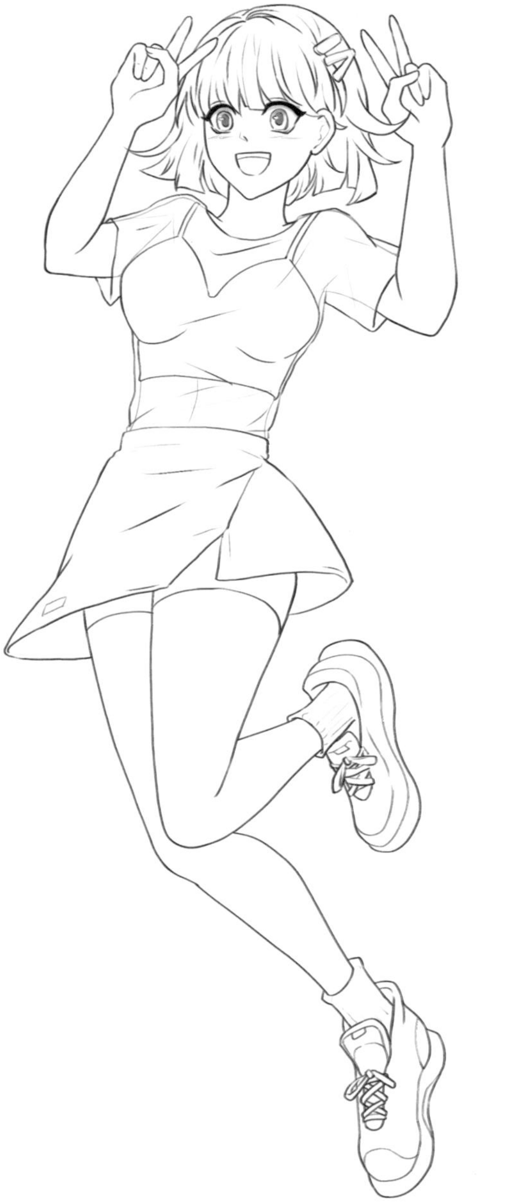

4

Outline the clothing, and pay attention to the way the clothes flare out and crease as they jump. Develop the facial features.

5

Complete your character with finishing touches to the face, hair, clothes and shoes.

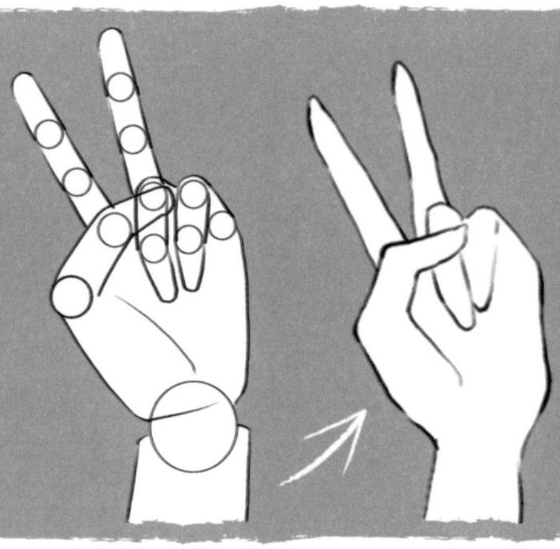

EXTRA DETAIL

To draw the 'V' signs, look closely at the distances between each joint. Fingers only bend where there are joints.

FORWARD CHARGE

This high-energy character is charging straight into the action. For added drama, give them a focused, determined expression.

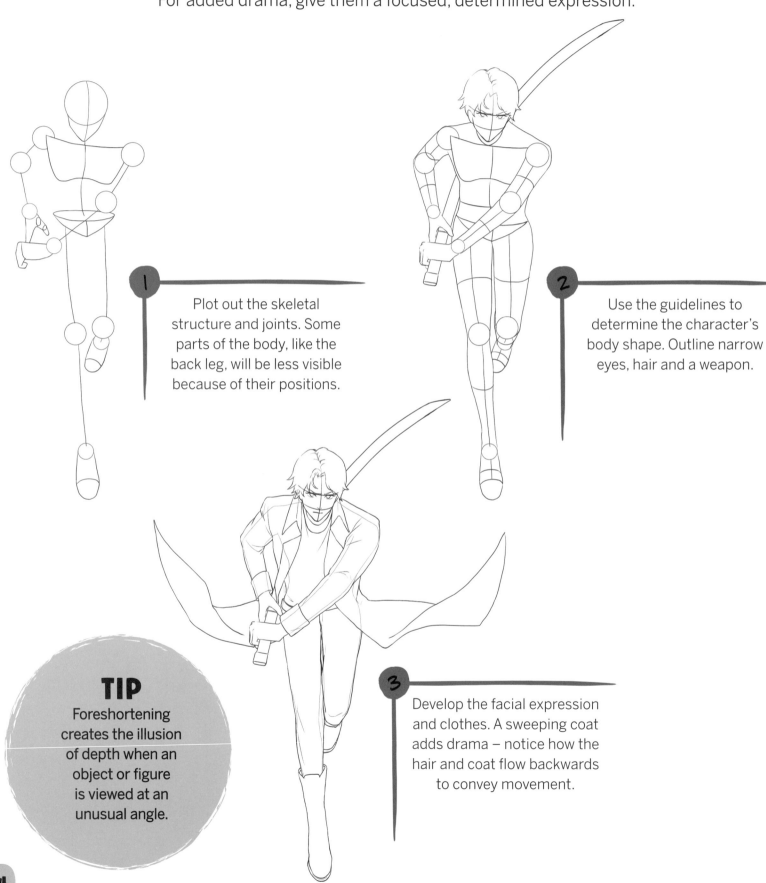

1

Plot out the skeletal structure and joints. Some parts of the body, like the back leg, will be less visible because of their positions.

2

Use the guidelines to determine the character's body shape. Outline narrow eyes, hair and a weapon.

3

Develop the facial expression and clothes. A sweeping coat adds drama – notice how the hair and coat flow backwards to convey movement.

TIP

Foreshortening creates the illusion of depth when an object or figure is viewed at an unusual angle.

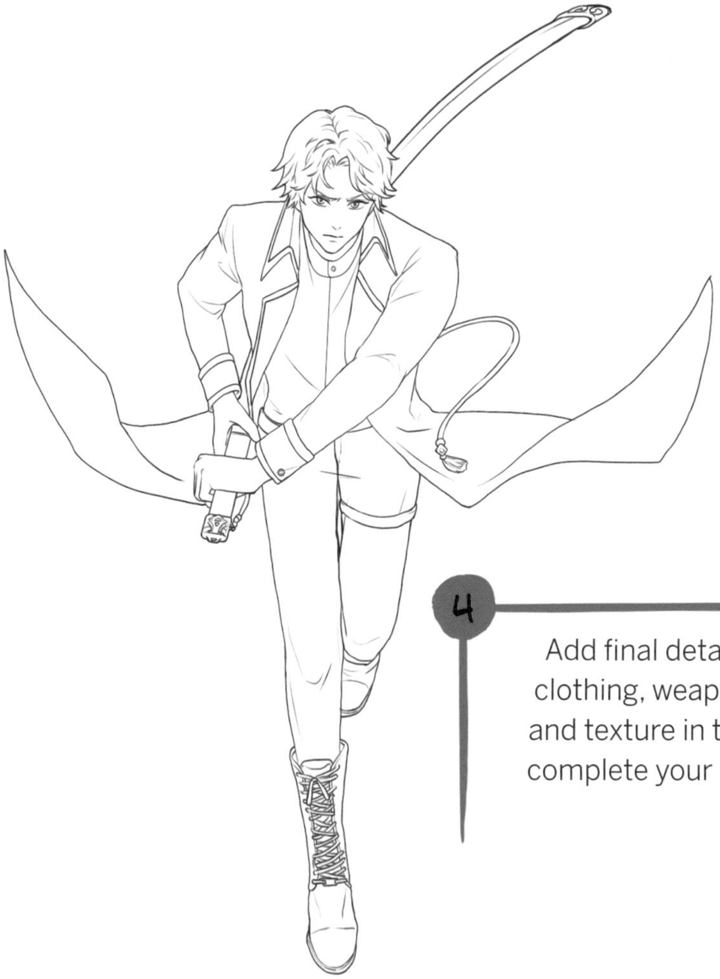

4

Add final details to the clothing, weapon, shoes and texture in the hair, to complete your character.

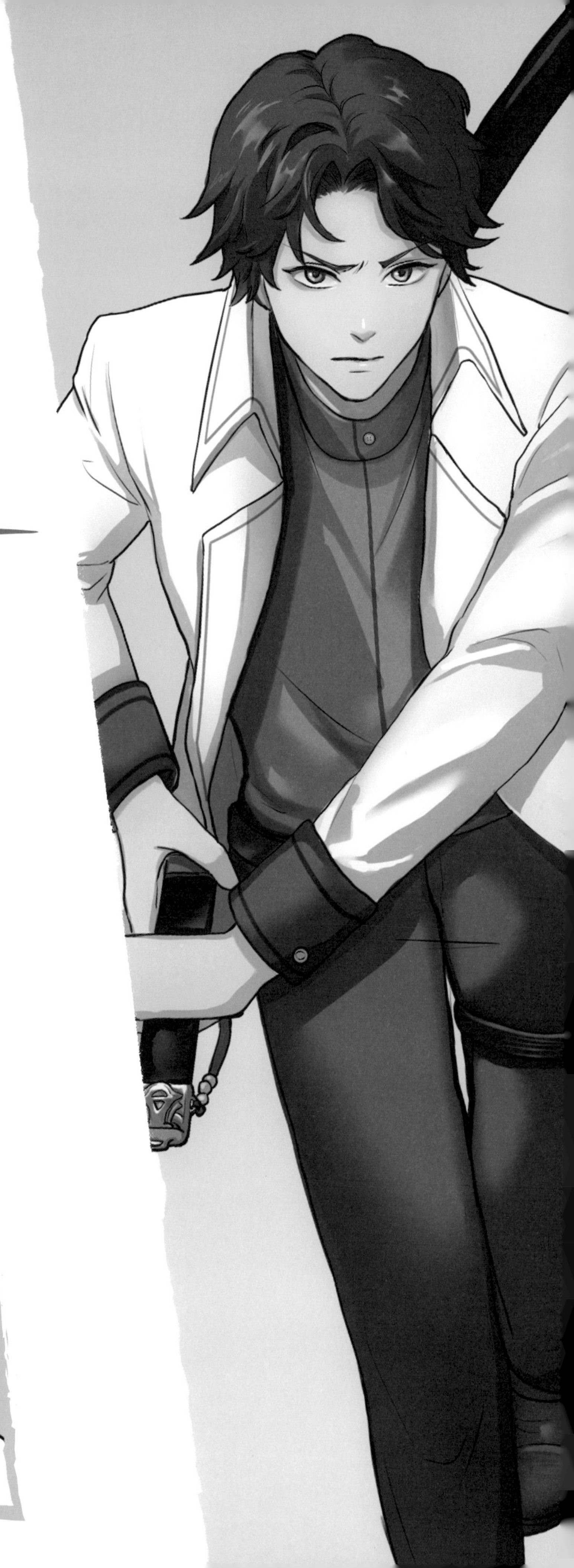

EXTRA DETAIL

For a determined expression, give your character a furrowed brow and thin line for a mouth, with the corners pointing down.

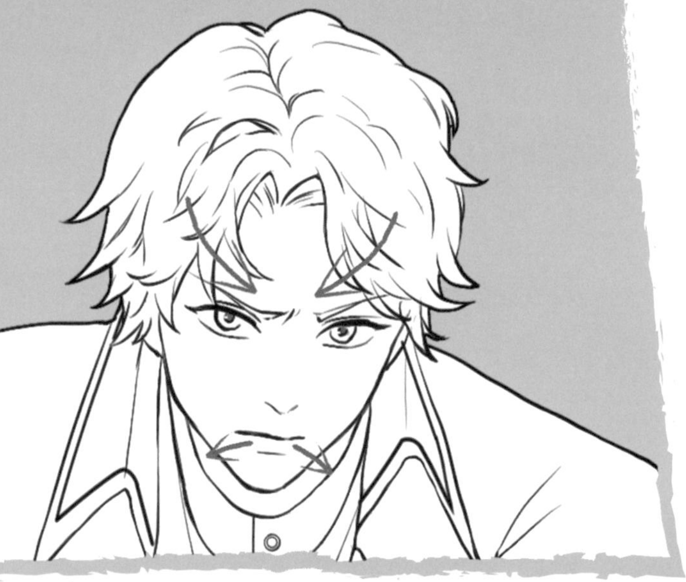

CHIBI STYLE

Standing just one to three heads tall, Chibi characters are less than half the size of regular manga figures. With oversized, distinct facial features, they lend themselves perfectly to cuter characters.

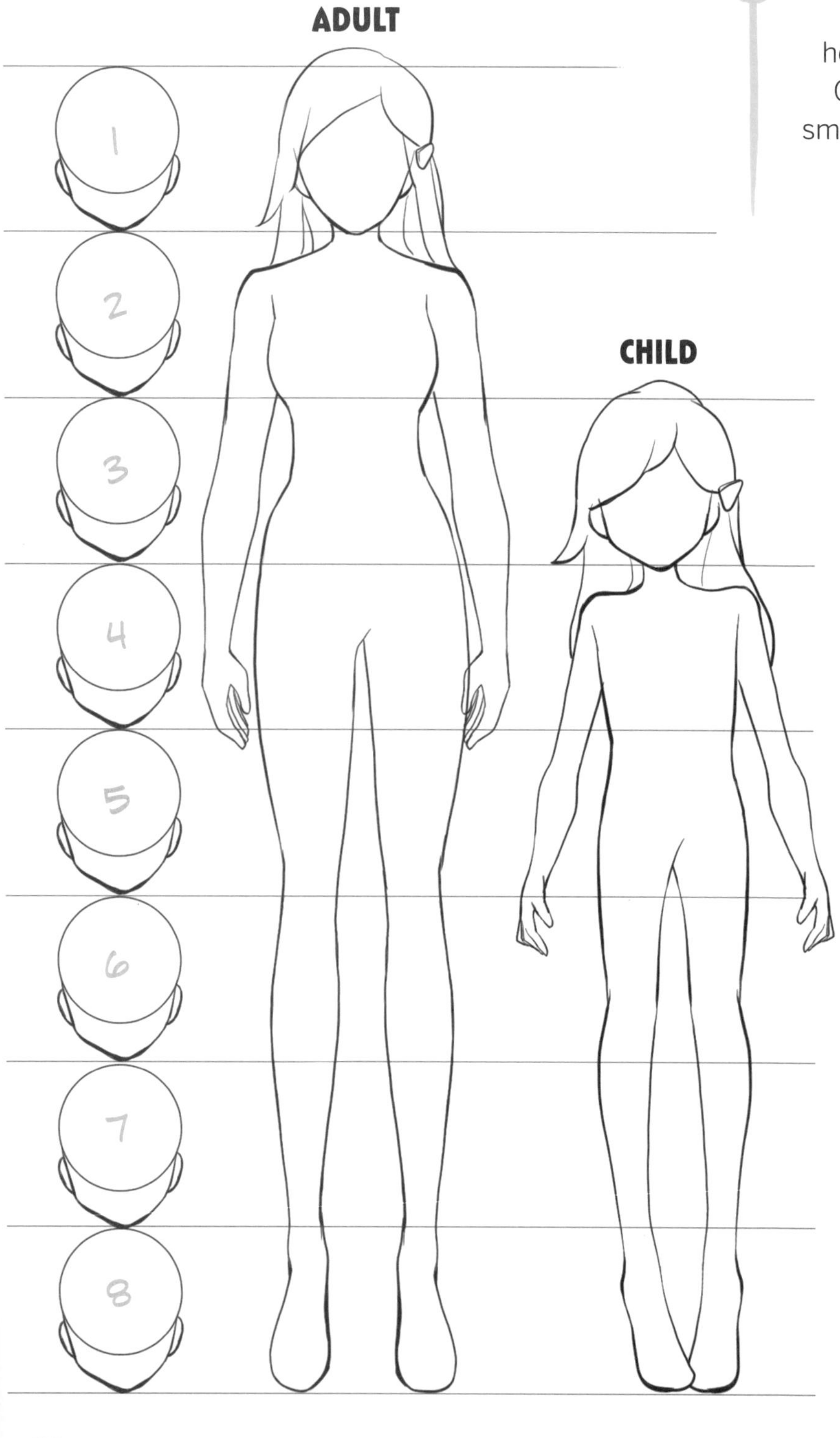
ADULT
CHILD
1
2
3
4
5
6
7
8

1

A typical adult figure is around eight heads tall. A child is around six heads tall. Chibi characters are disproportionately smaller, at just one to three 'Chibi' heads tall.

TIP
Chibi characters tend to have fewer features that are more exaggerated.

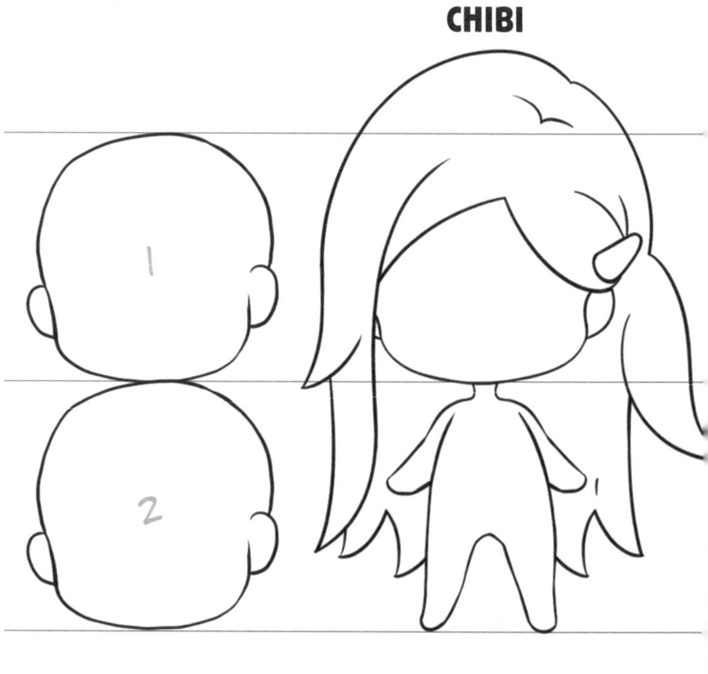
CHIBI
1
2

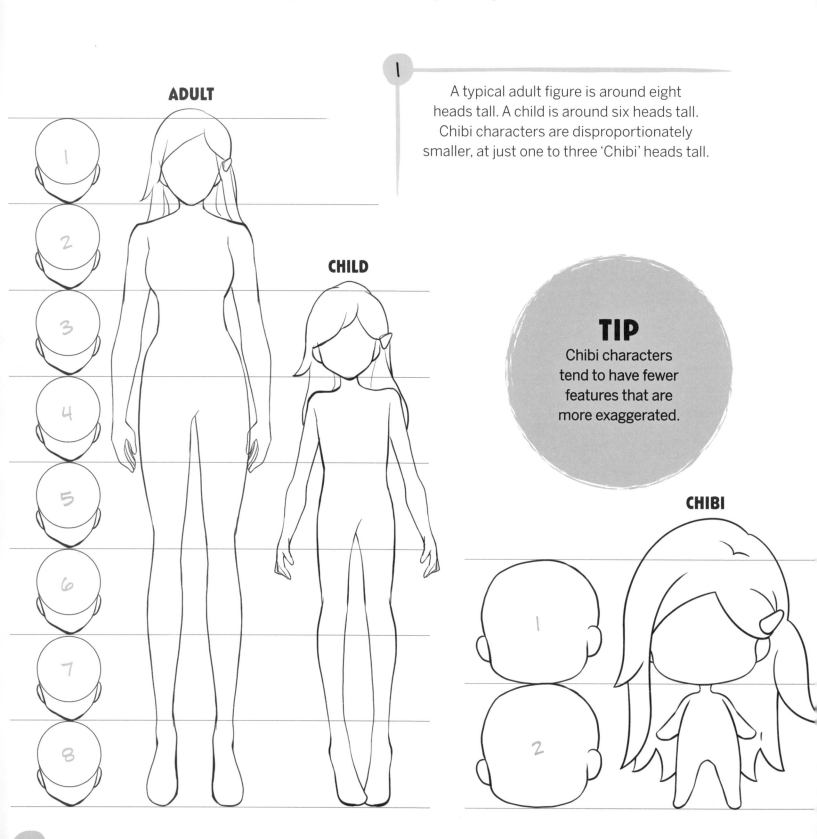

1

Sketch out the miniature frame. The head is roughly the size of the rest of the body combined.

2

Add structure to your character, fleshing out the body. Sketch in the face with large, exaggerated eyes.

3

Sketch a hairstyle and outfit. This character's bunches and pinafore give it a young, cute appearance.

4

Add details and accessories. A floppy straw hat and large flower help to reveal personality.

5

Finish off any final details, for example, adding texture to the straw hat.

CHIBI CHARACTERS

While Chibi characters always have small bodies, they come in all shapes and sizes. Experiment with different proportions to see what suits your character best.

WAITRESS

Chibi characters vary in size. The head to body ratio ranges from super short, with the head and body roughly the same size, to slightly taller, where the body may be twice the size of the head.

PUNK

Whether a Chibi character is scaled up or down in size, the head stays approximately the same size in each version.

SASSY PERFORMER

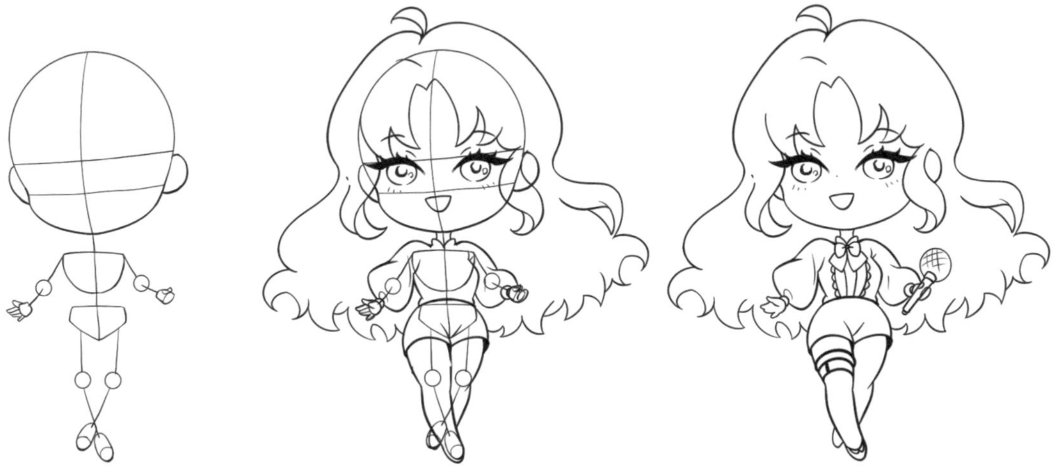

Chibi-size characters give a different impression to full-size people. This sassy performer's head is about the same size as the rest of her body combined.

TEEN REBEL

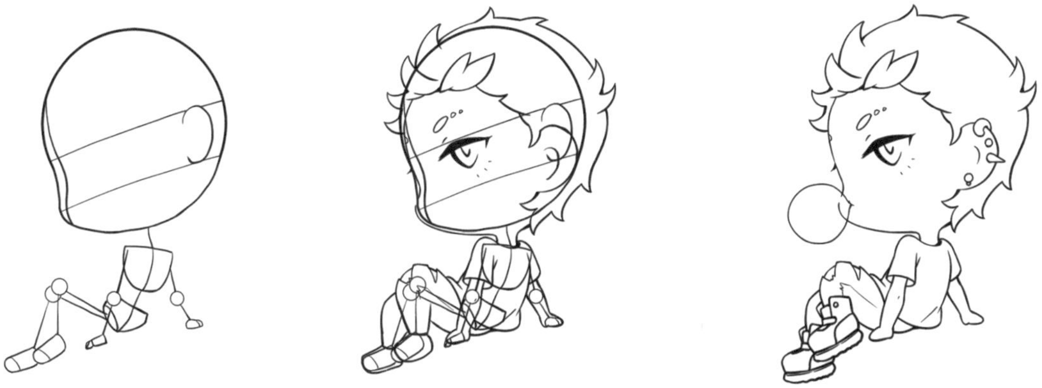

Focus on exaggerated facial features. Add a hairstyle and accessories to suit your character's personality. Piercings and chewing gum suit this rebellious teen character.

MARTIAL ARTIST

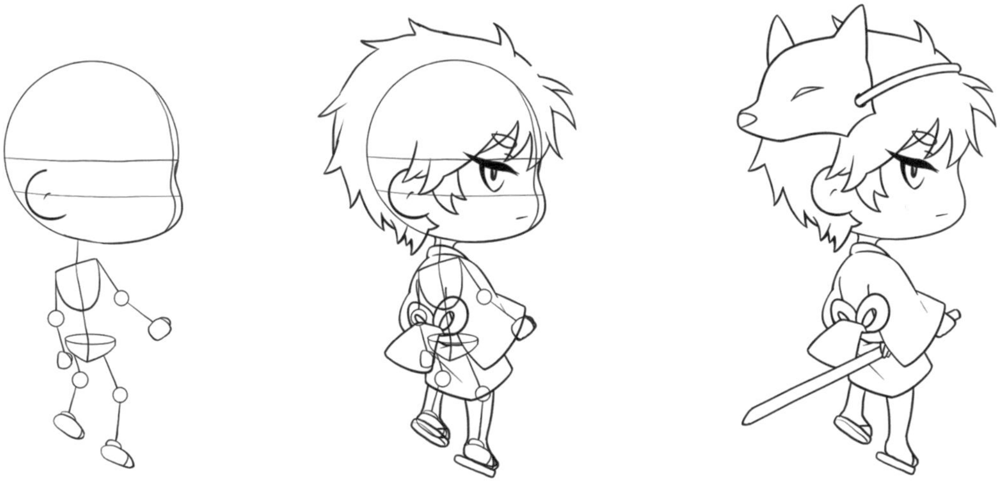

Choose a pose that suits the personality of your character – they may be self-assured or turning away, bashfully. If you add colour go extra bright to make the Chibi features pop.

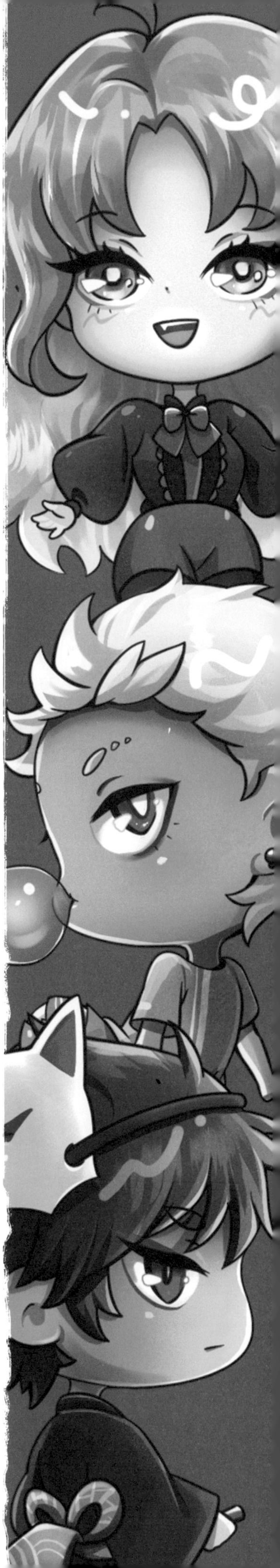

CREATURE COMPANIONS

Cats and dogs are among the most loved creatures on Earth. Both animals walk on four legs – they are 'quadrupedal' – unlike humans, so pay attention to their anatomy as you draw.

CAT

1

Begin with a rough sketch, plotting where the limbs, joints and key facial features fall. Reference images such as photographs may help you approach the animal's anatomy.

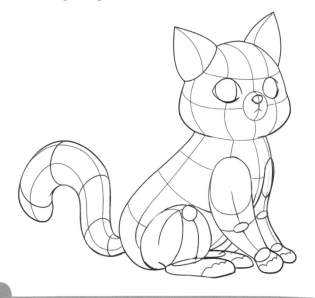

2

Build the cat's shape and sketch the eyes and mouth, using the guidelines. Feel free to experiment with proportions, making the ears and eyes larger to enhance its cuteness.

3

Refine your lines, and develop the ears, nose and expression. Is your cat playful, cheeky or aloof?

4

Give the cat's coat texture, adding tufts of fur around the ears, tail and legs. Add details to the face, reflections to the eyes and give your character some quirky accessories.

DOG

1 Start by sketching a pose, using reference images for guidance. You may want to enlarge the eyes and head to make your dog look cute and stylized.

2 Develop the body's dimensions, using the guidelines. This dog has a rounded appearance, so the guidelines should be curved. Sketch the eyes, as shown.

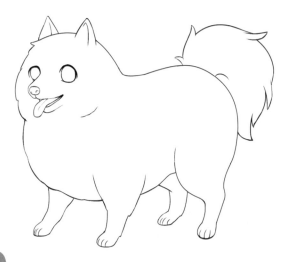

3 As you develop the face, tail and ears, think about how the dog's character can be revealed through its expression and features.

4 Refine the lines, adding details to the face, tufts of fur and accessories to bring out your dog's charm. The fur could be short and fluffy, as here, or long and silky.

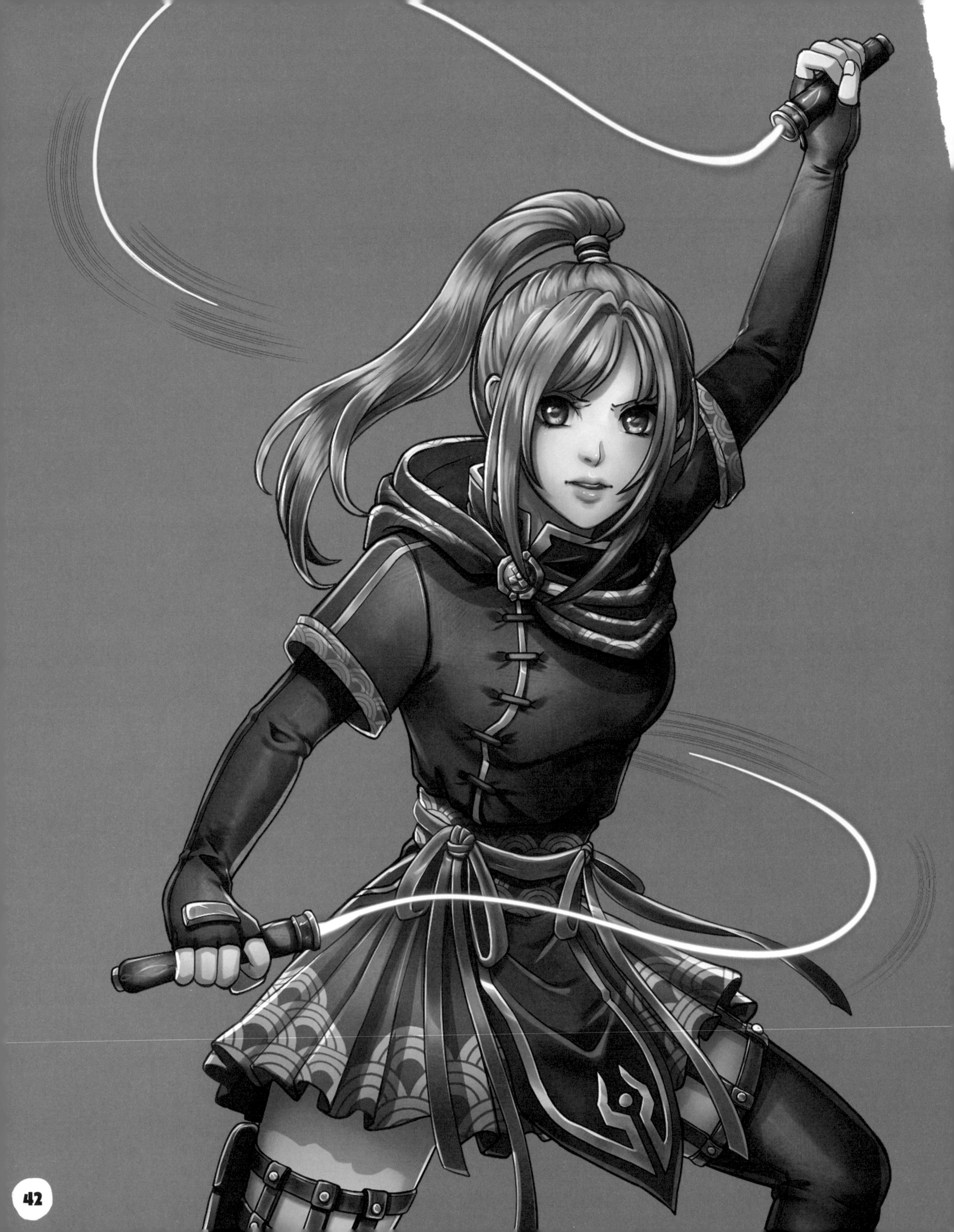

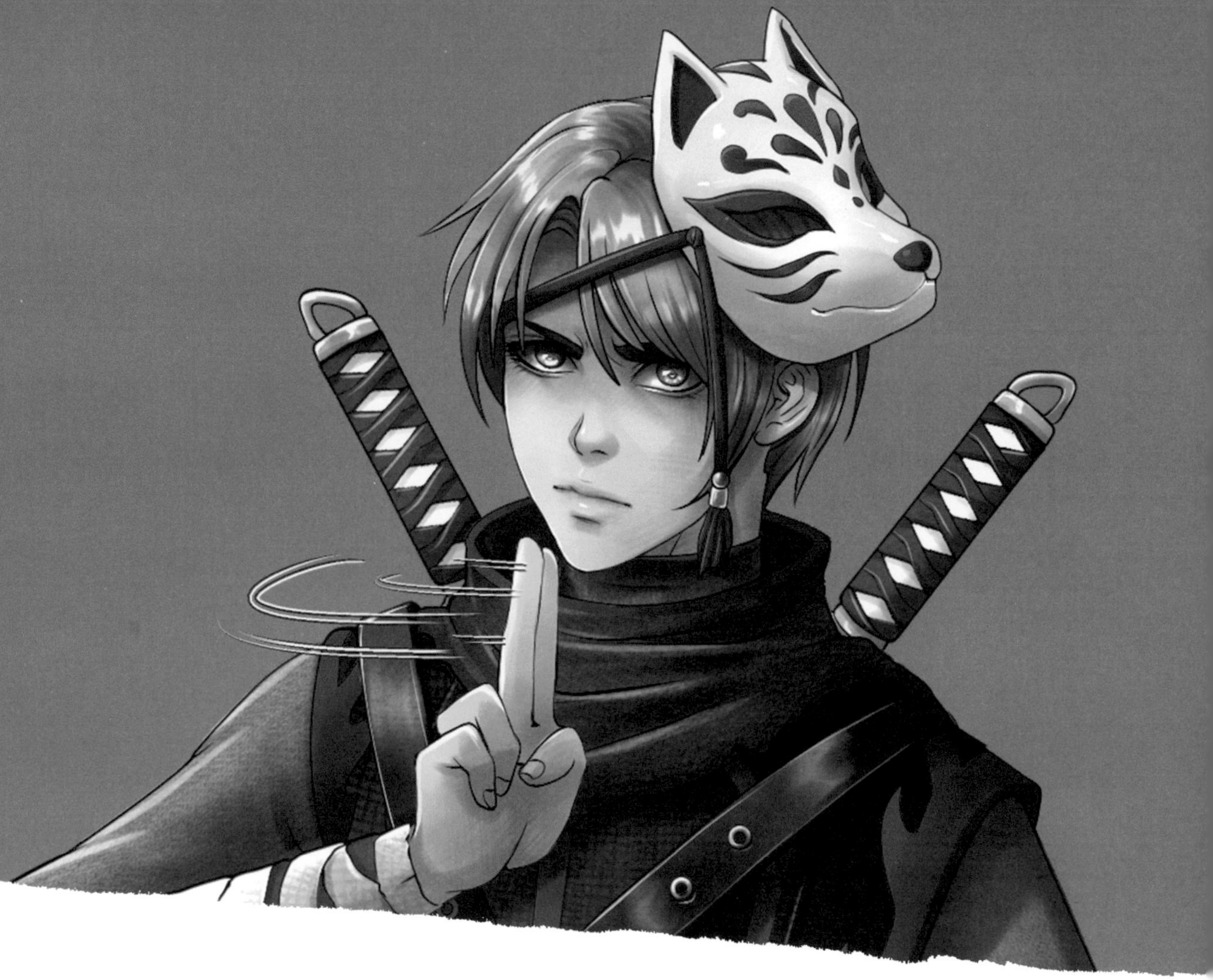

HEROES AND VILLAINS

No graphic novel is complete without its heroes and villains. Take your drawing skills to the next level, designing sporting heroes, magic-wielding sorcerers, lightning-fast ninjas and loyal sidekicks. Give your characters weapons, accessories, special effects and even make them fly.

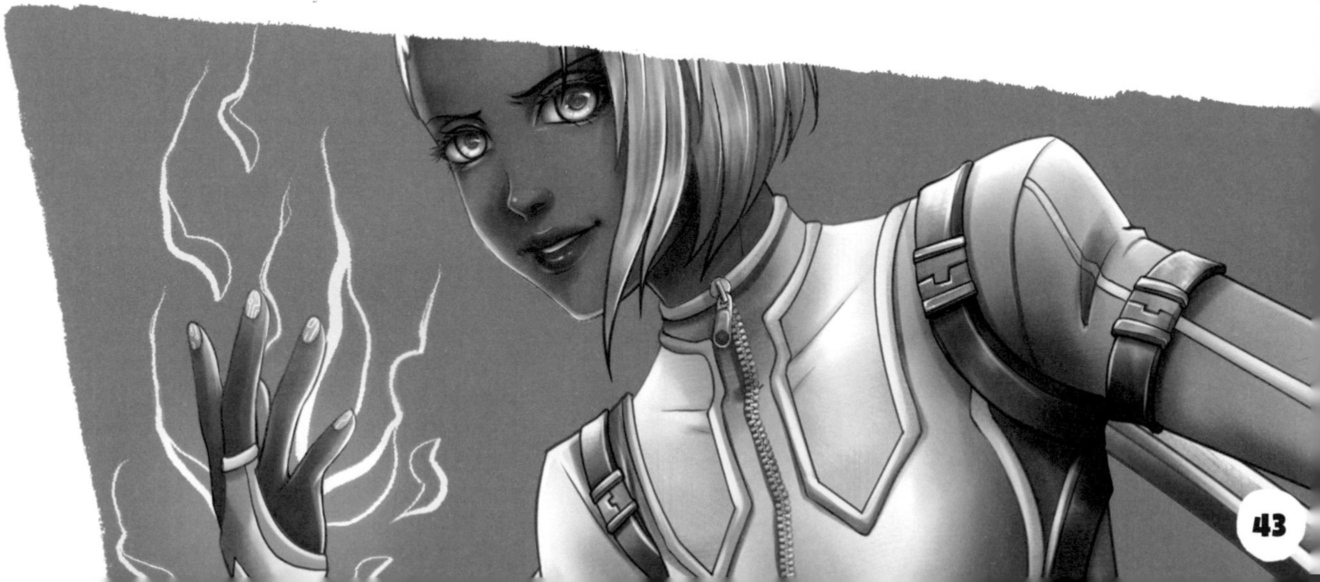

BASKETBALLER

This basketballer is focused on winning the game. Pictured mid-jump, with bent legs and one arm outstretched to reach the ball, he gives an active, determined impression.

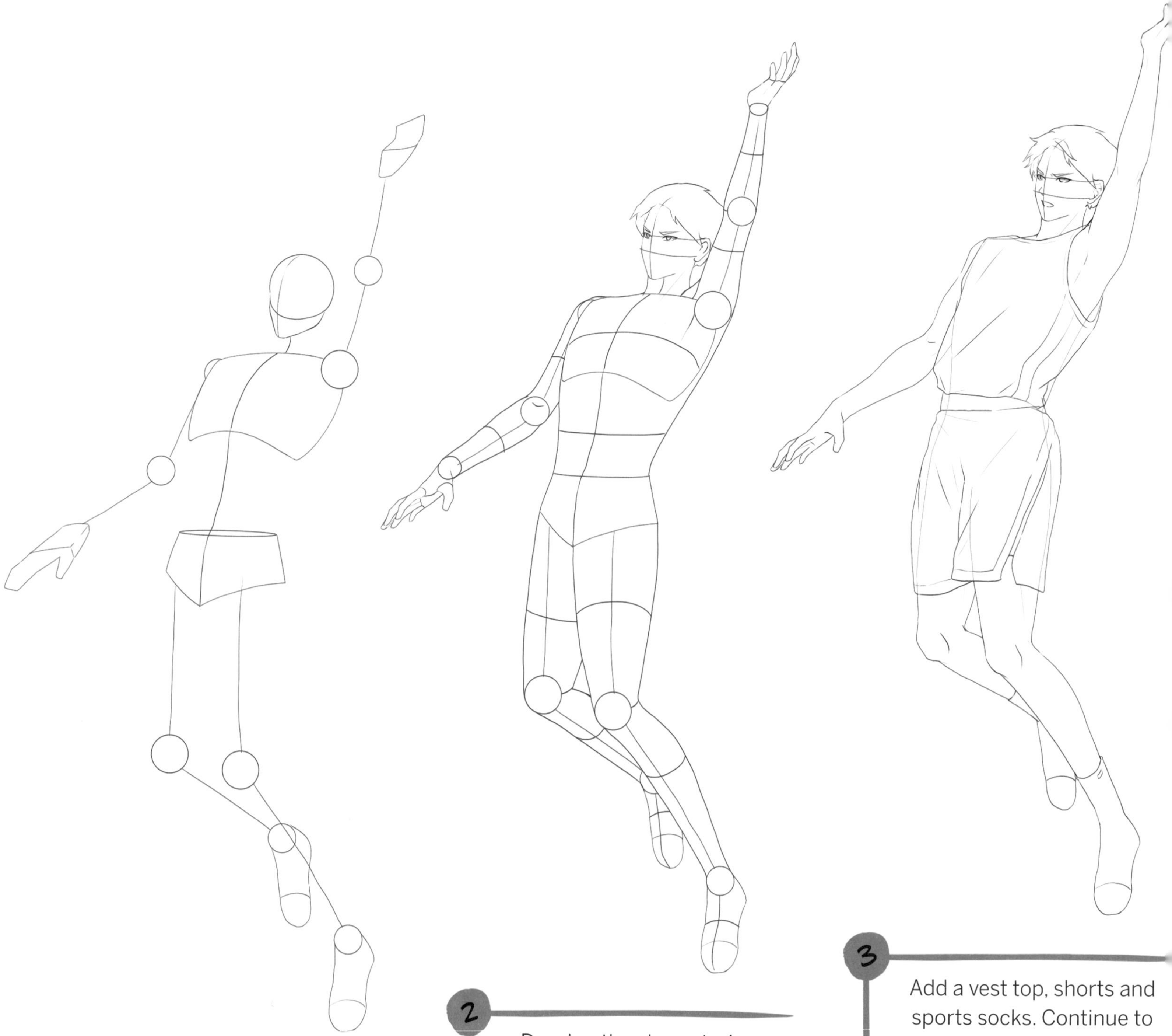

1

Sketch the skeletal structure and joints. This character is leaping into the air.

2

Develop the character's lean build and sketch the hair. The eyes are narrow and the brow is furrowed.

3

Add a vest top, shorts and sports socks. Continue to add the facial features, giving your character a determined expression.

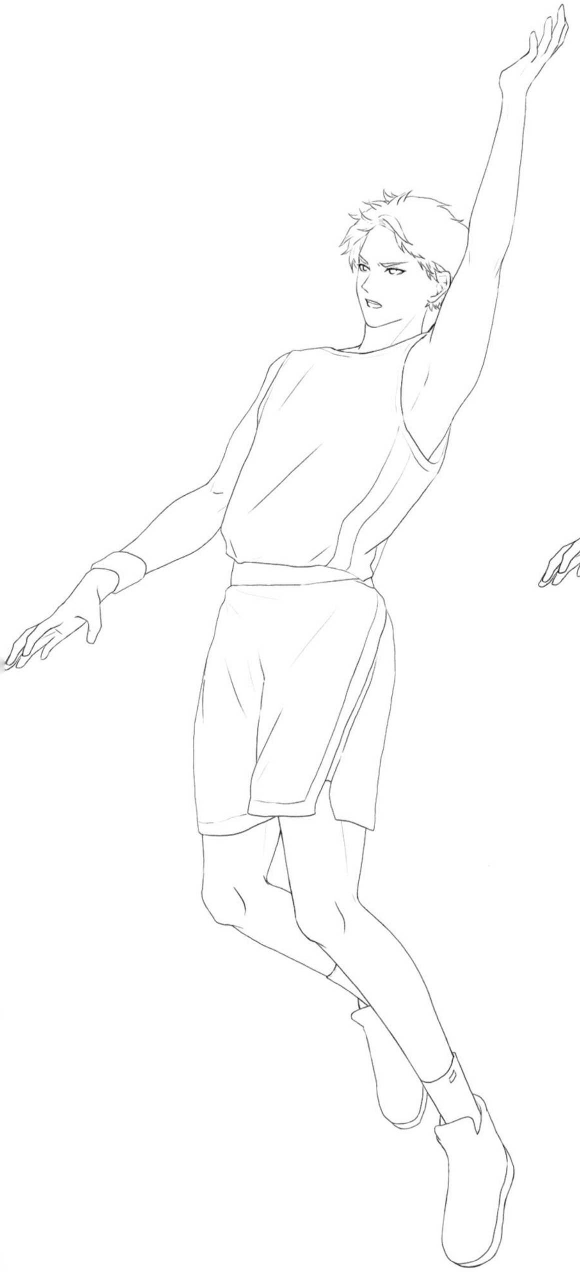

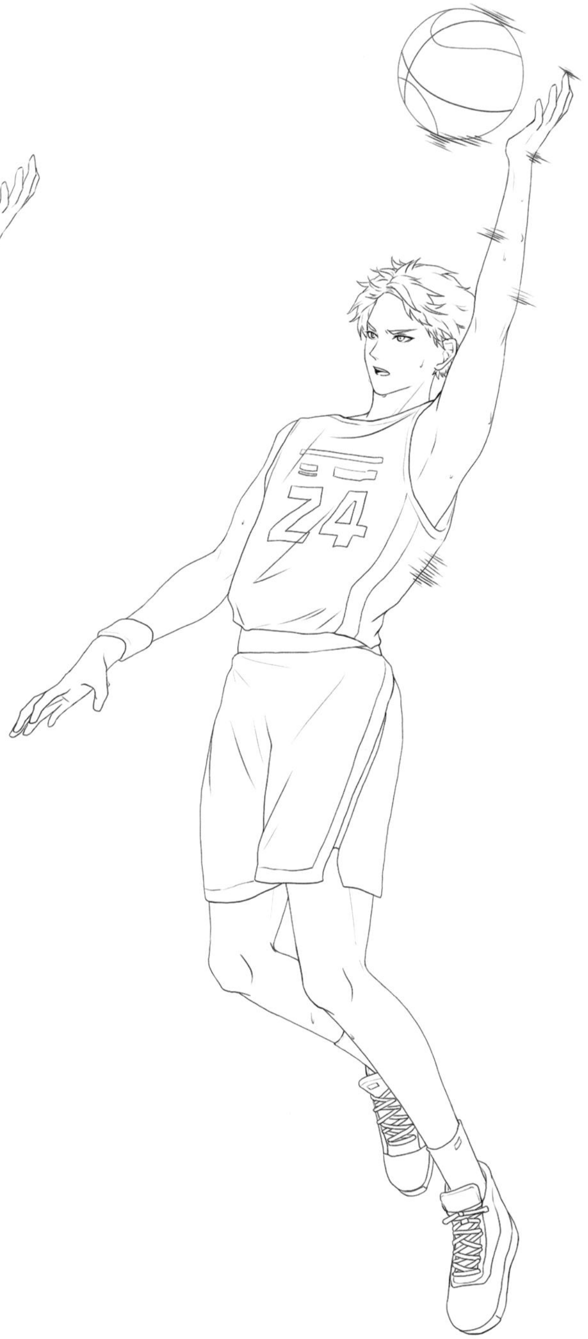

4

Sketch in sports shoes and a wrist band. Develop the creases on the clothes to give the impression of movement.

5

Add a number to the shirt and a basketball to play with. Finish the details on the shoes, face and hair, and add motion blur to convey movement.

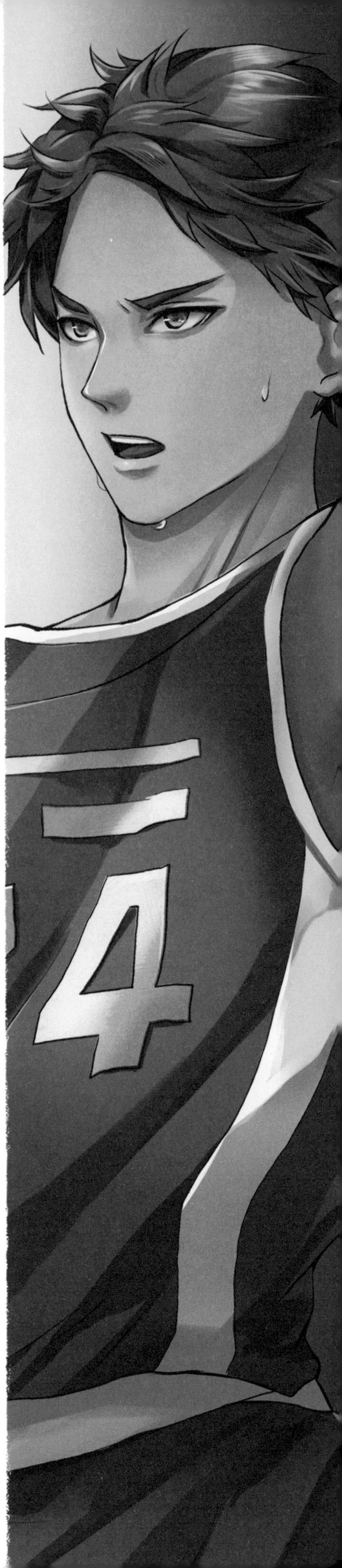

NINJA GIRL

Ninjas, also known as 'shinobi' (those who act in stealth), are well-loved for their incredible combat abilities. This ninja holds a strong, battle-ready stance.

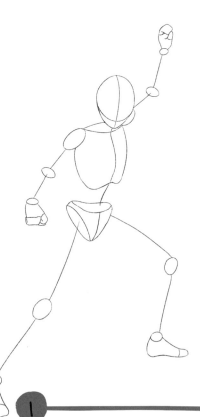

1 Sketch your ninja's skeleton and joints. The active positions of the limbs give the impression of movement.

2 Flesh out the body and use guidelines to determine your ninja's robust, athletic build. Sketch in the whips.

3 Outline your character's eyes and hair. Dress them in simple, lightweight clothing to enable agile movement, and develop the whips.

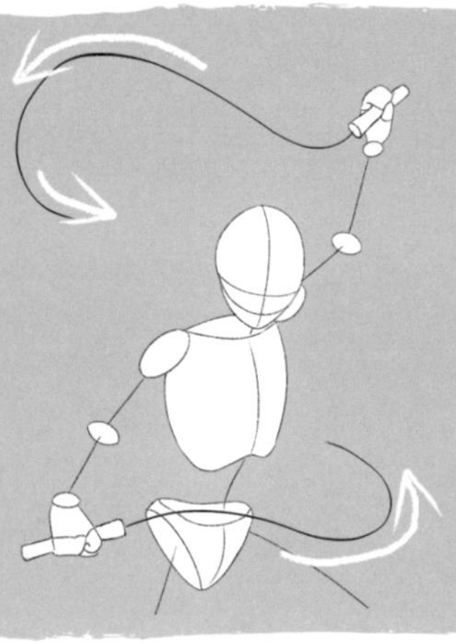

EXTRA DETAIL

The curved shapes of the whips emphasize the direction of their movement, as they are swung by the ninja.

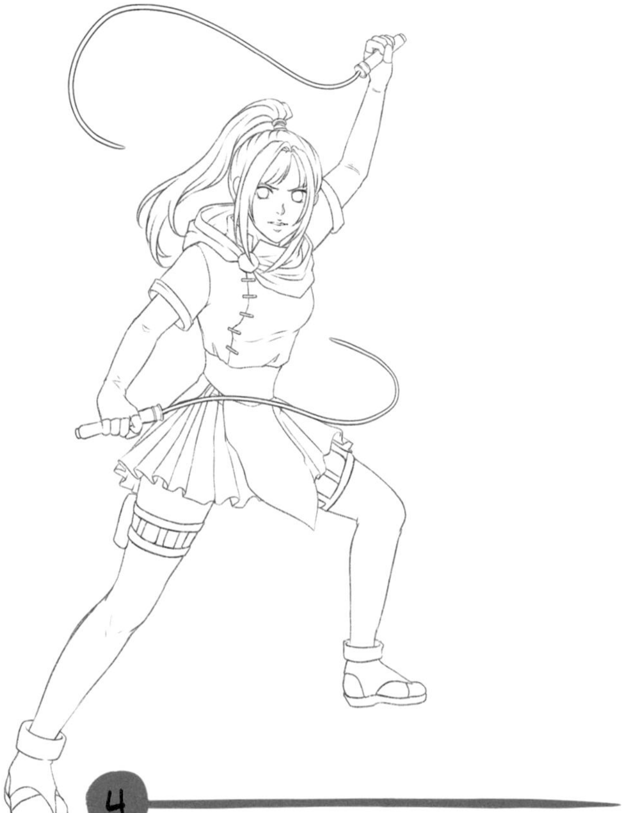

4

Give your character a fierce expression, fitting for a deadly ninja. Add details such as a hood, belt or sash and pleats to the skirt.

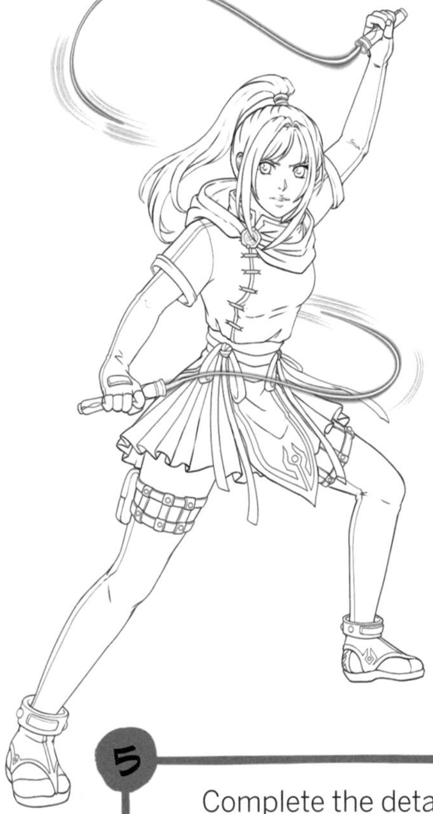

5

Complete the details on the clothes, shoes and face, including reflections in the eyes. Add motion blur to show the whips' speed.

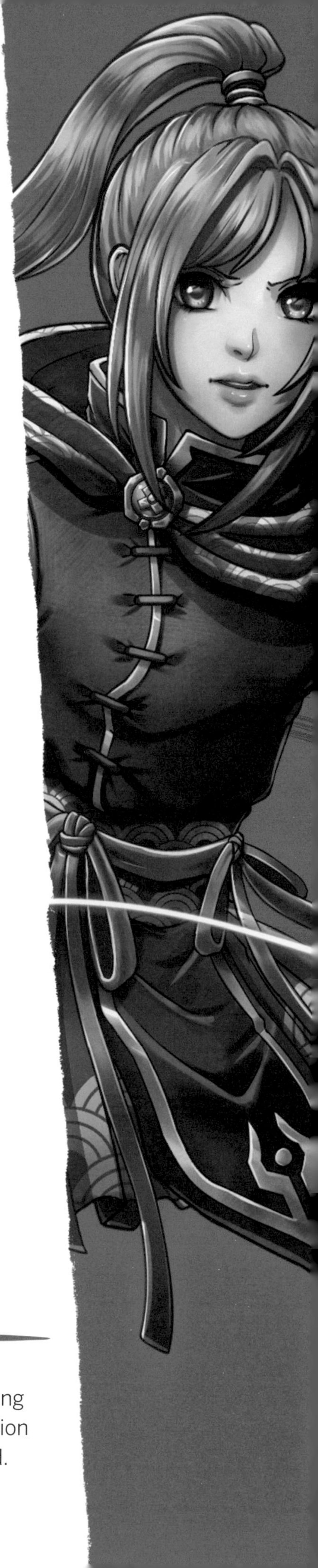

SORCERER

Learn to draw a young wizard in training, levitating above the ground. What can you add to reveal their character; are they practising magic for good or evil?

1 This magical character is sitting cross-legged, while floating effortlessly in the air. Sketch the skeleton and joints to show this.

2 Build your character's body around the guidelines. Outline the eyes and add an unruly mop of hair.

3 Develop your character's serene facial expression and add the clothing. A cloak and pointy hat are essential for a witch or wizard.

4 Embellish with decorative details and creases to the clothing. Finish with enchanted floating paper, sparkles and wispy magical tendrils.

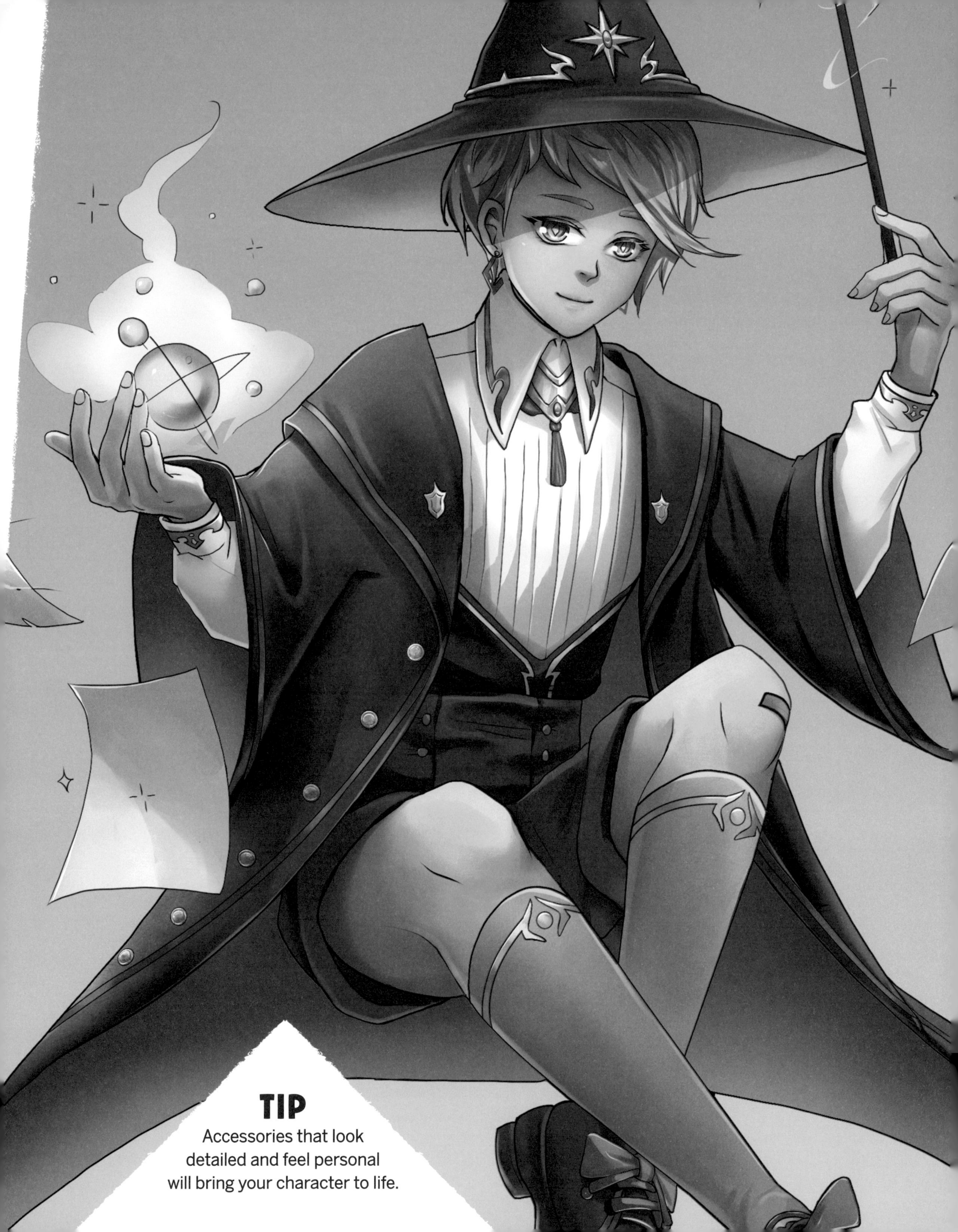

TIP

Accessories that look detailed and feel personal will bring your character to life.

FLYING SUPERHERO

Create your own superhero with unique superpowers and a bold, sculpted outfit to match. They could have the ability to fly, climb walls or shoot lightning from their fingertips.

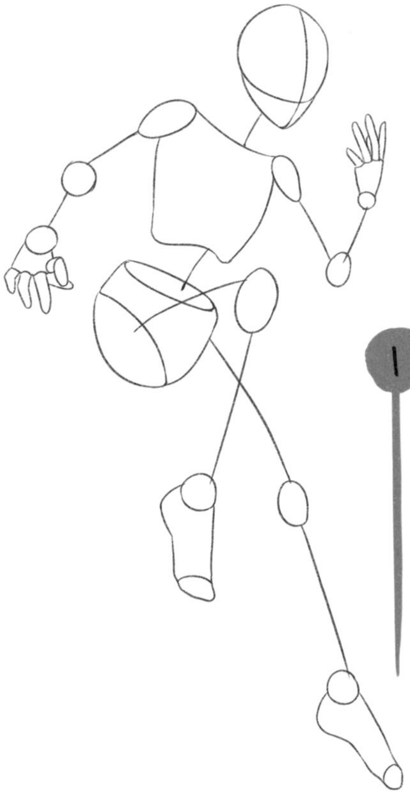

1

Start with the skeletal frame and joints for the torso, arms and legs to get a clear idea of movement in the pose. This character is flying.

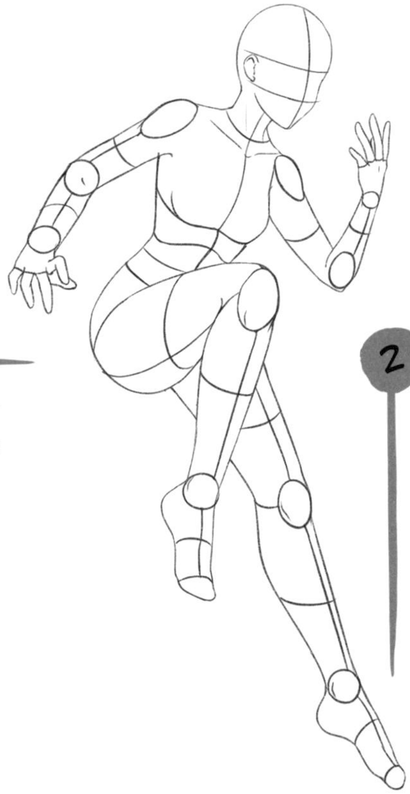

2

Define your character's build with the use of the guidelines and flesh out the body.

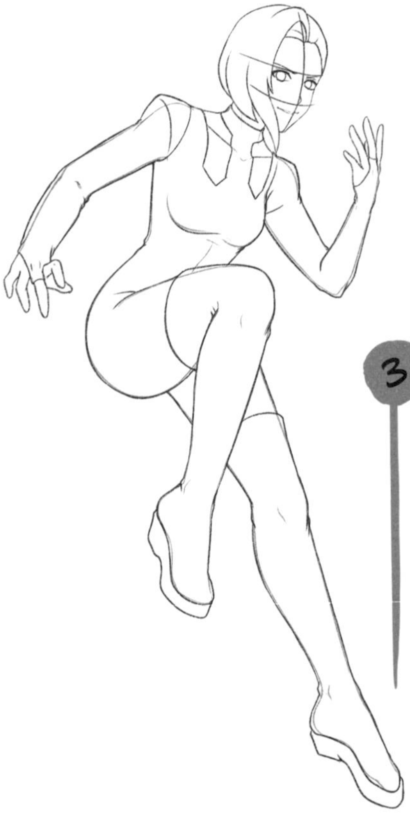

3

Add facial features and a cool hairstyle. Outline an outfit; superheroes typically wear sleek, form-fitting costumes.

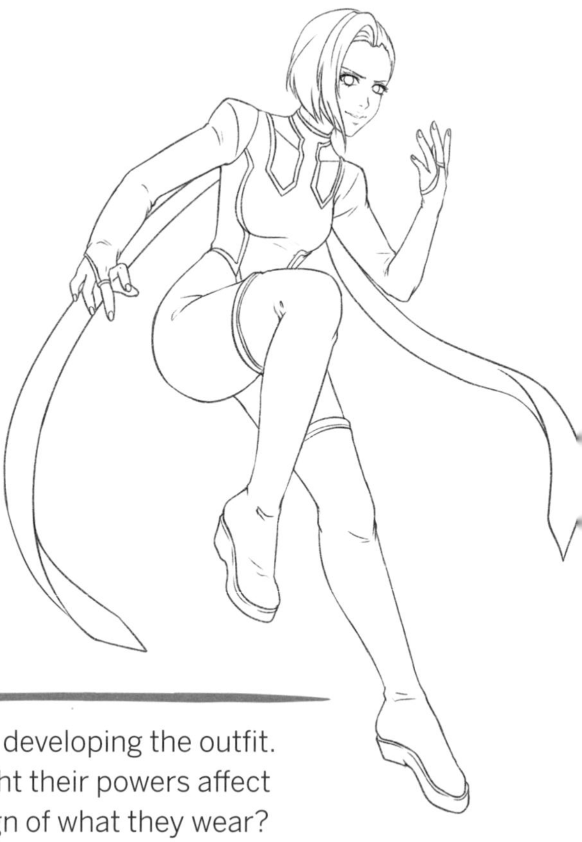

4

Continue developing the outfit. How might their powers affect the design of what they wear?

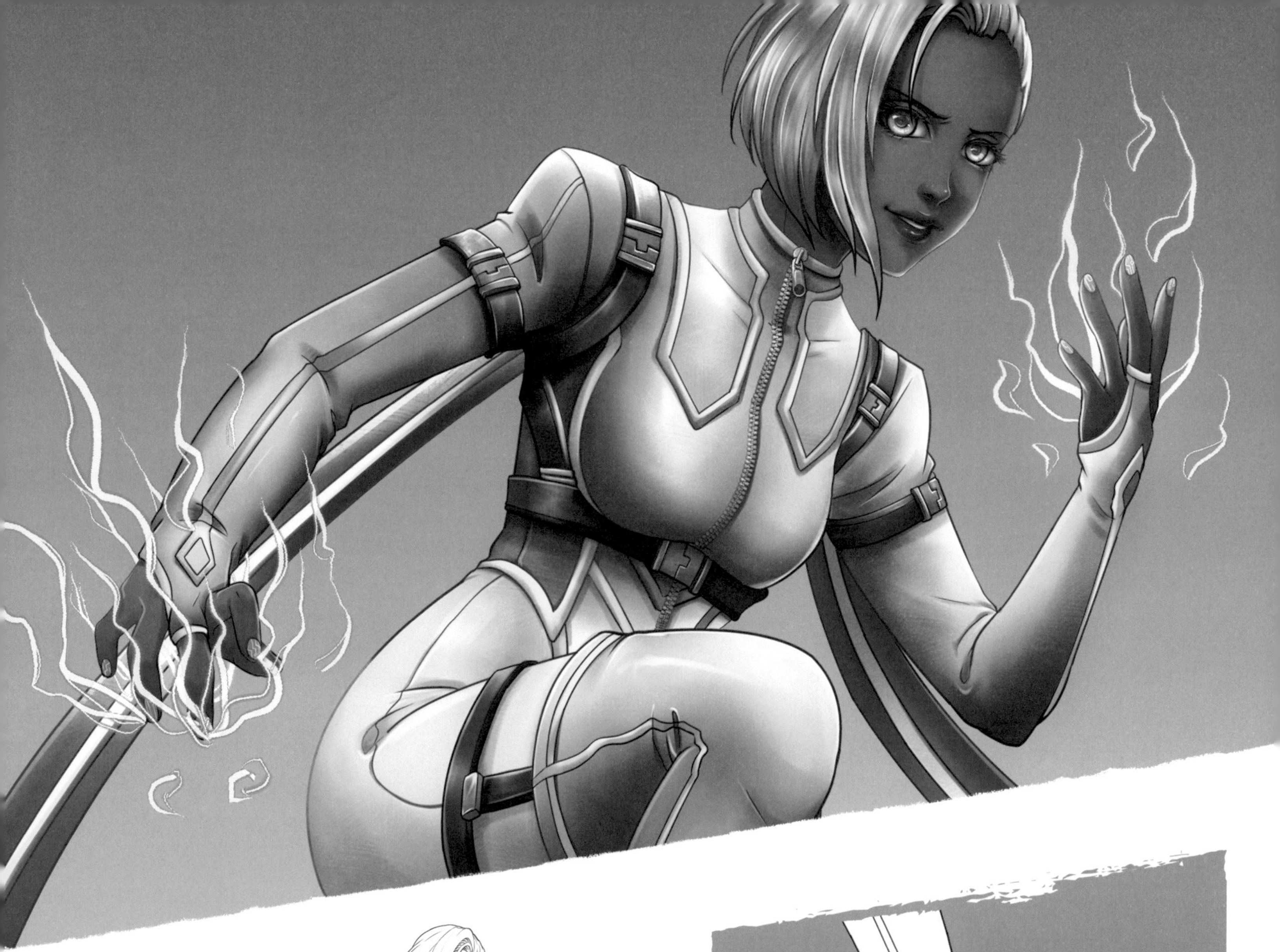

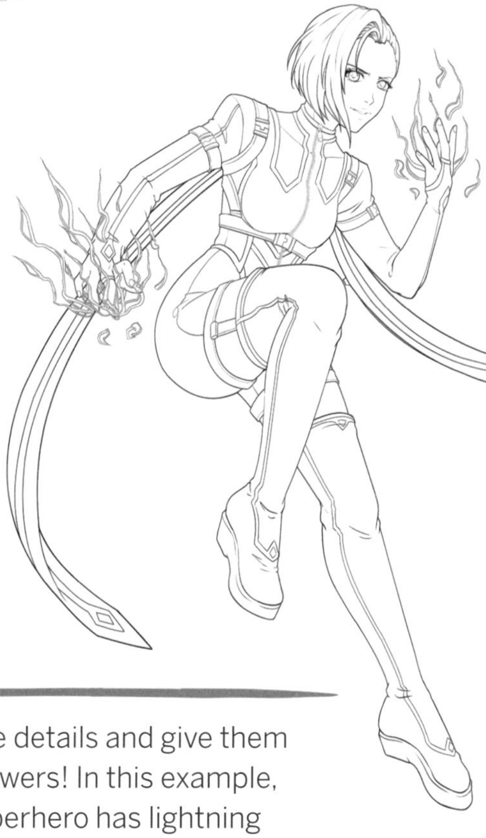

5

Finish the details and give them superpowers! In this example, the superhero has lightning smouldering at their fingertips.

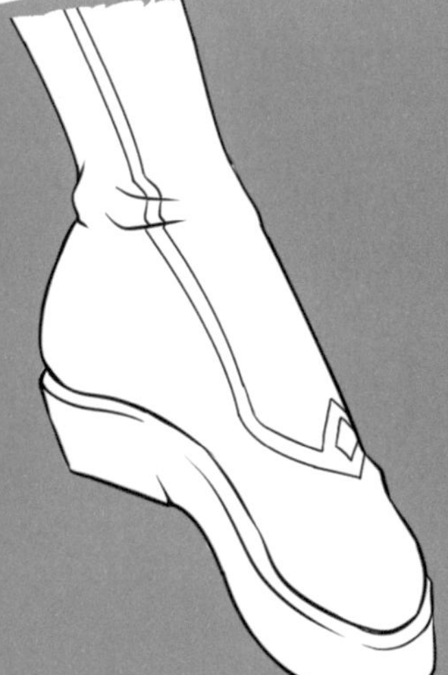

EXTRA DETAIL

Want to give your superhero the gift of flight? Draw the toes pointing down to make your character look like they're effortlessly rising above the ground.

NINJA BOY

For this character design, consider the physical and mental posture, or 'kamae', of the ninja. These stances are used in Ninjutsu (martial arts practised by ninjas) to help gauge distance and orientation.

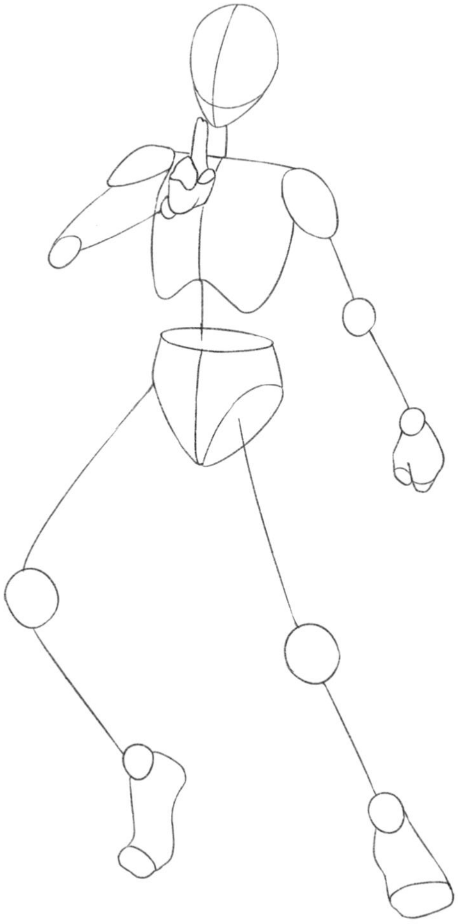

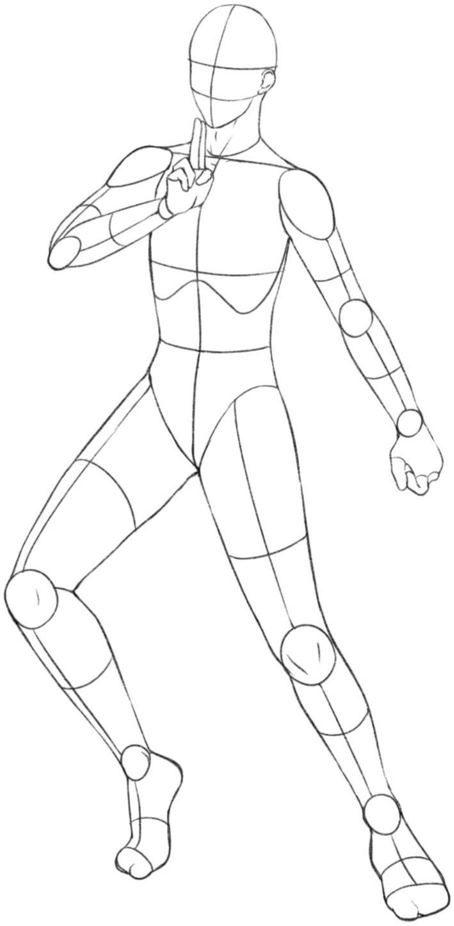

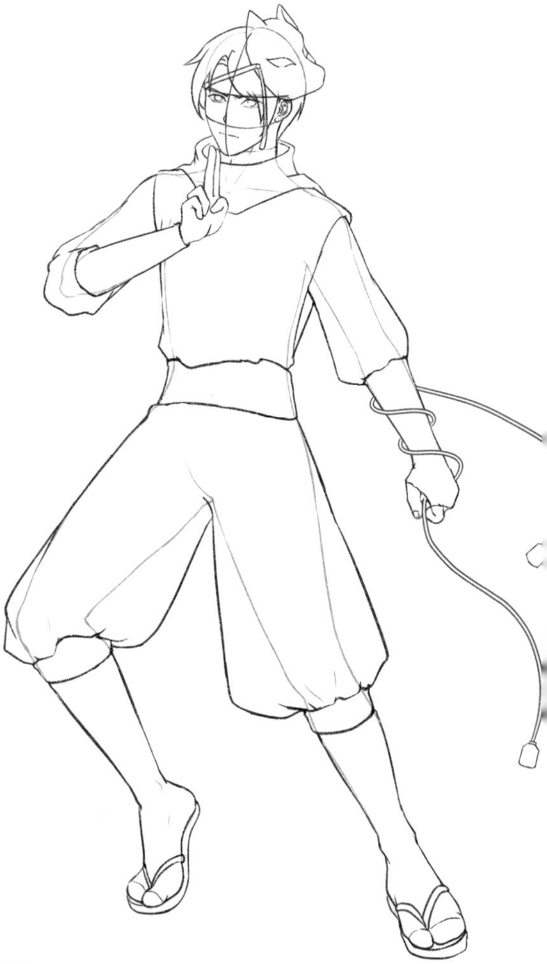

1

Begin by sketching the skeletal structure and joints. The pose above is a typical ninja stance (kamae).

2

Develop your ninja's build and flesh out the body. They may have a lithe, athletic build due to years of combat practice.

3

Traditionally, ninjas wear black jackets, trousers, sandals and a large, loose covering around the neck or head, called a 'cowl'. Sketch the face and chain whip. Make your ninja more unique by adding a 'Kitsune' (fox) mask.

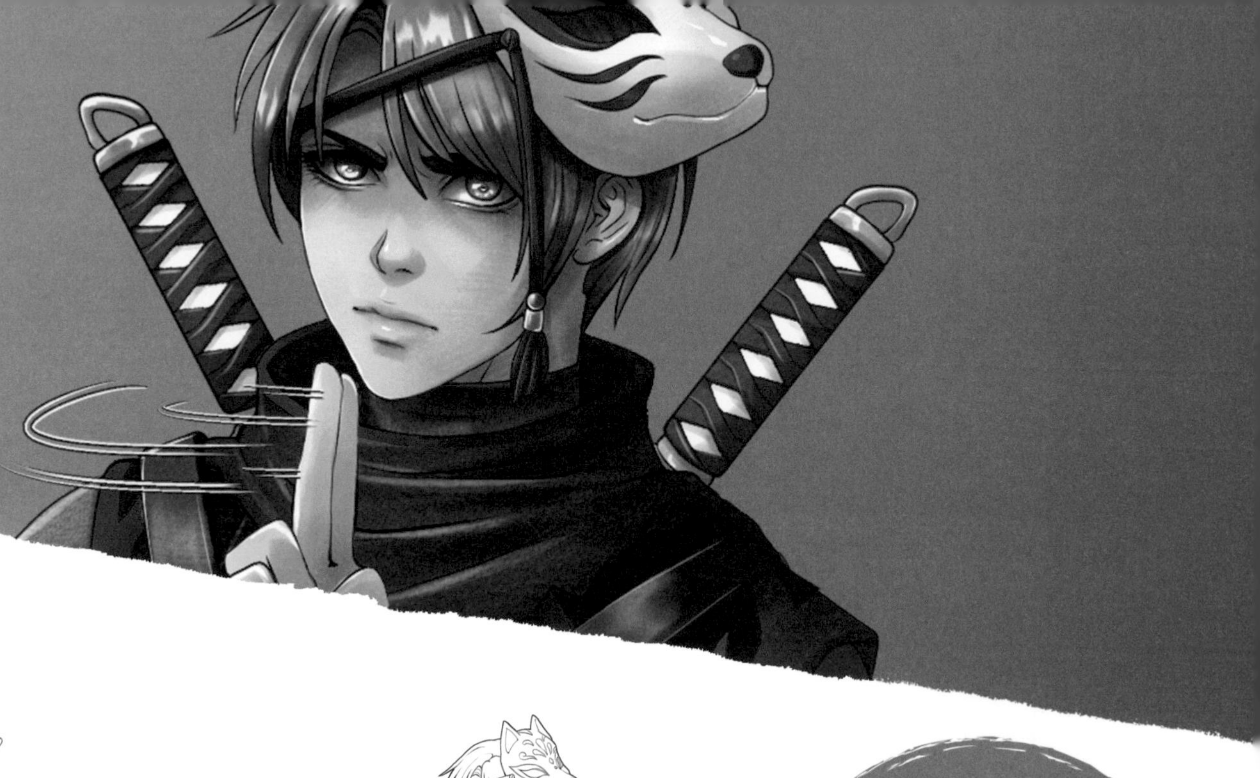

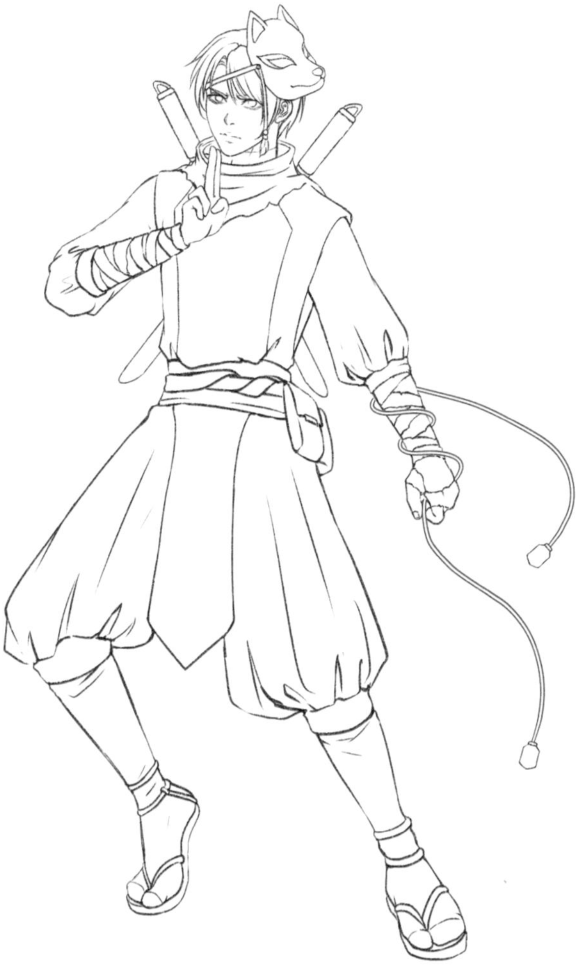

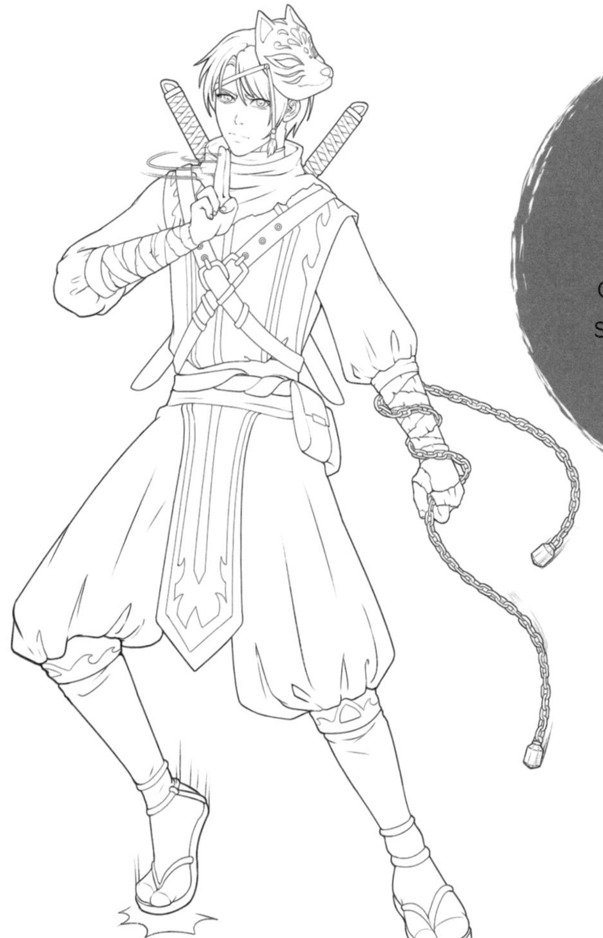

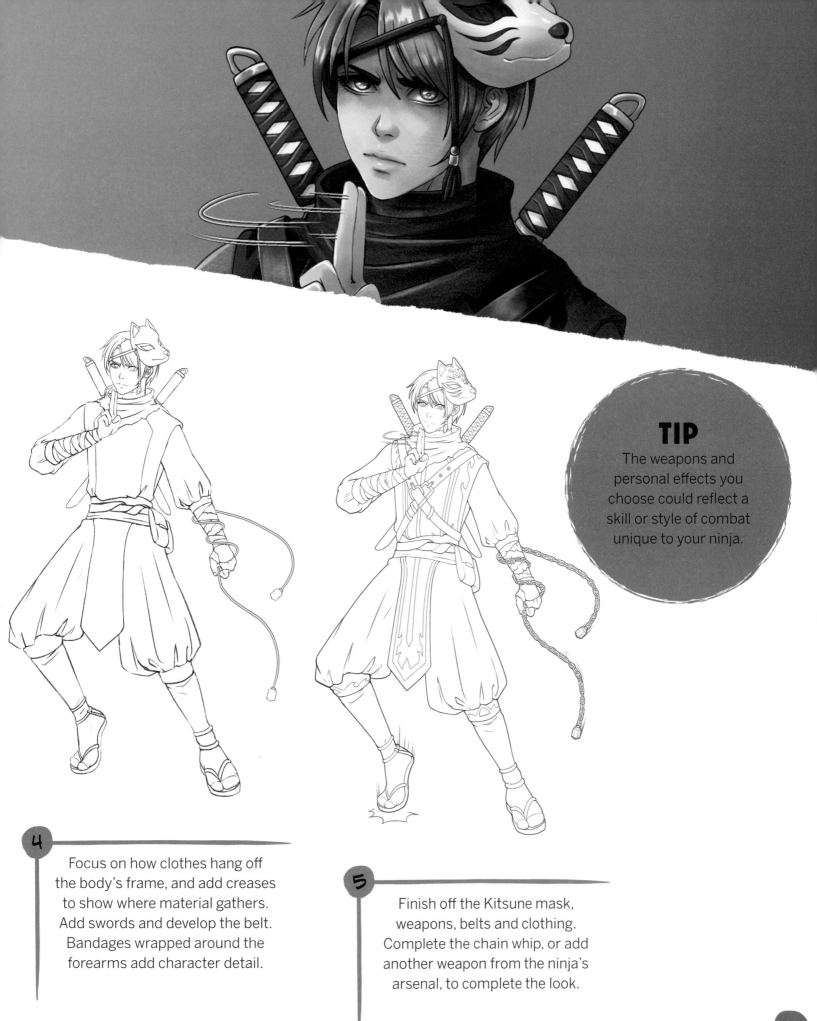

TIP

The weapons and personal effects you choose could reflect a skill or style of combat unique to your ninja.

4

Focus on how clothes hang off the body's frame, and add creases to show where material gathers. Add swords and develop the belt. Bandages wrapped around the forearms add character detail.

5

Finish off the Kitsune mask, weapons, belts and clothing. Complete the chain whip, or add another weapon from the ninja's arsenal, to complete the look.

YATAGARASU

A ninja's sidekick is a close, faithful companion who may hold intrinsic wisdom and is essential to the character they accompany. The three-legged crow Yatagarasu originates from East Asian mythology and is known for its sharp eyesight, intelligence and wise guidance.

1 Use reference images of birds to help you understand their anatomy. Don't miss the Yatagarasu's third leg when sketching this basic skeletal structure and joints!

2 Use guidelines to flesh out the form and outline the wing and tail feathers. You may prefer to sketch each leg separately to break down the process, before adding them to your Yatagarasu.

3 Use fluid, sweeping lines to develop the body and wings. The feathers should look strong yet supple.

4 Add any final details, such as markings, accessories and motion blur lines (see page 59), to enhance your Yatagarasu's character.

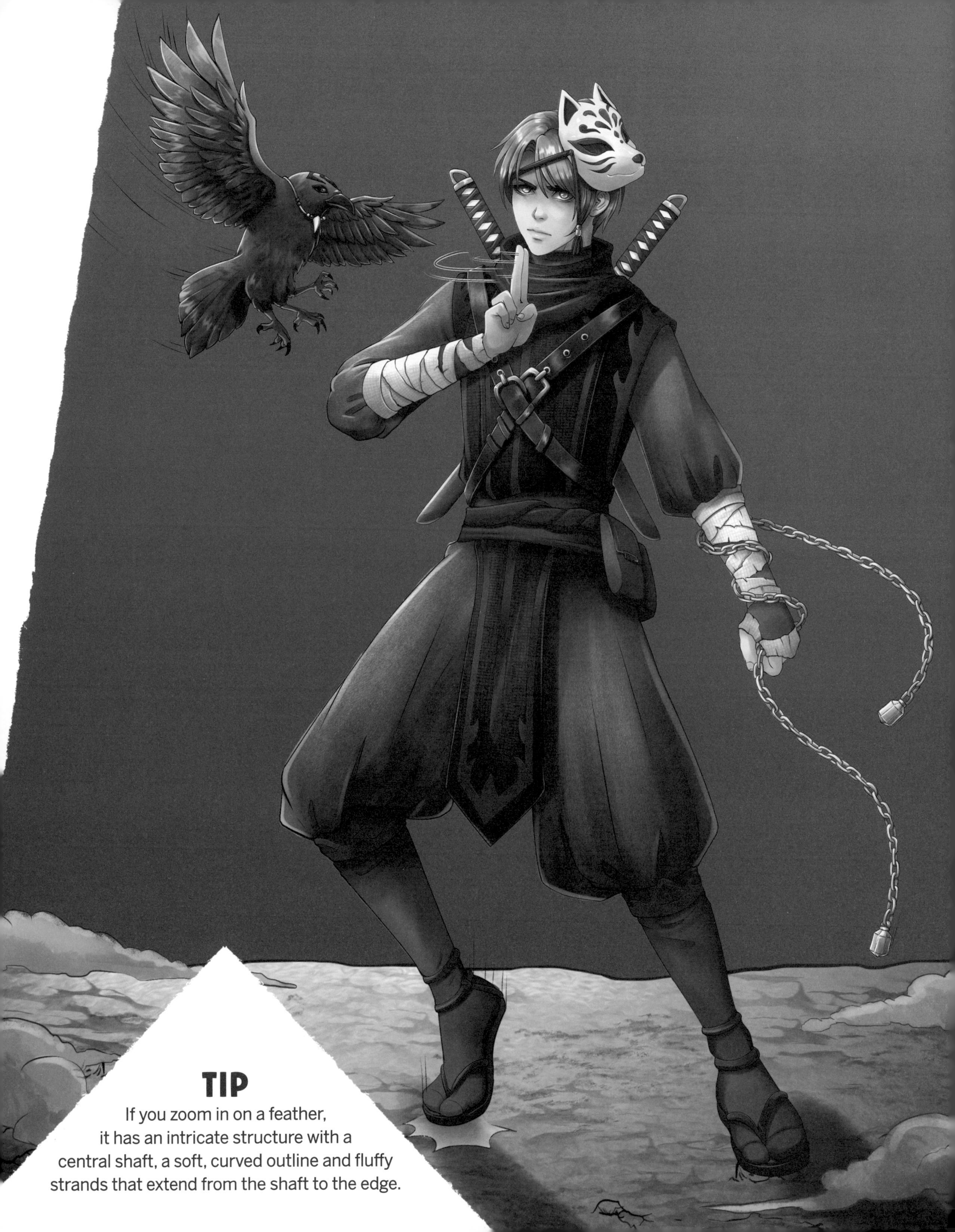

TIP

If you zoom in on a feather, it has an intricate structure with a central shaft, a soft, curved outline and fluffy strands that extend from the shaft to the edge.

GEEK CHIC

A classic manga character trope, these modest geeks or underdogs are full of surprises. They may look timid, but rest assured, they can transform from zero to hero in an instant.

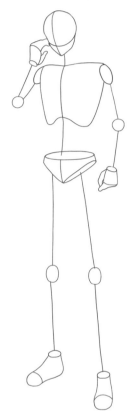

SCHOOLBOY

1 Begin with the skeleton and joint structure. A hand raised to the face makes your character appear a little self-conscious.

2 Sketch the eyes and develop the character's build, using the guidelines. Given their 'geek' status, you may choose a less muscular frame.

3 Outline the hair and clothing. This outfit is based on school uniform, complete with a smart blazer.

4 Finish the schoolboy look with a tie and satchel. Add final details to the face and uniform, and make the hair feel unruly by detailing individual strands and adding shading.

SCHOOLGIRL

1

Plot the skeleton and joints in a simple pose. With a slightly hunched posture, this character gives the impression that they prefer blending into the background.

2

Develop your character's build. Sketch a loosely tied hairstyle and outline the eyes.

3

Design an outfit for your character. School uniform may suit the part, but feel free to add unique touches. Notice how the skirt swishes to one side, capturing a sense of movement.

4

Finish off the details. Large, round glasses, a hair band, cute bow and a school bag complete the look.

MARTIAL ARTIST

Martial arts are about more than just fighting and can be practised for many reasons, including fitness, spirituality and as part of rituals. The martial artist here performs an iconic 'hand beckoning' stance to taunt her opponent.

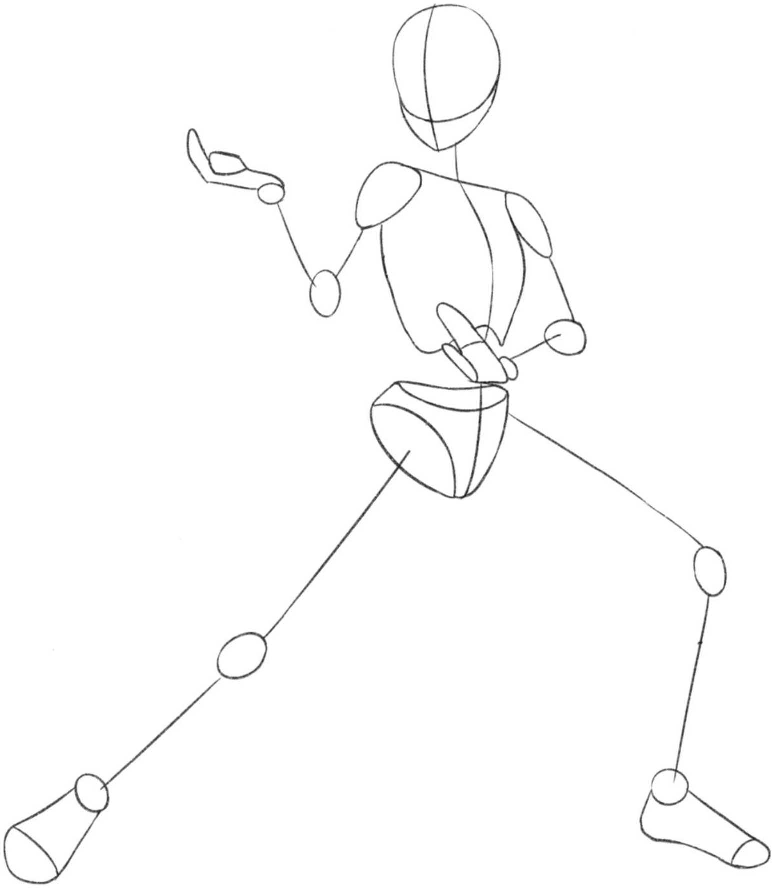

1

Sketch the skeletal frame and joints. Martial artists move with grace and speed – the pose should look balanced, as if it is performed with ease.

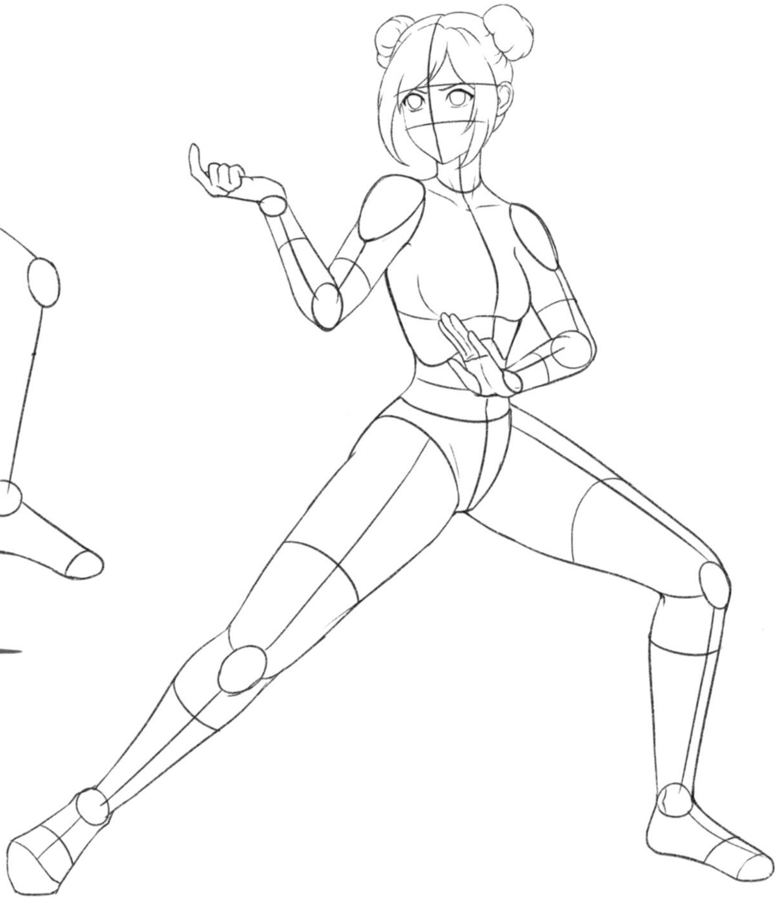

2

Flesh out the body, using the guidelines. Is your martial artist serious, serene, angry or taunting? Develop a facial expression, starting with the eyes and hair.

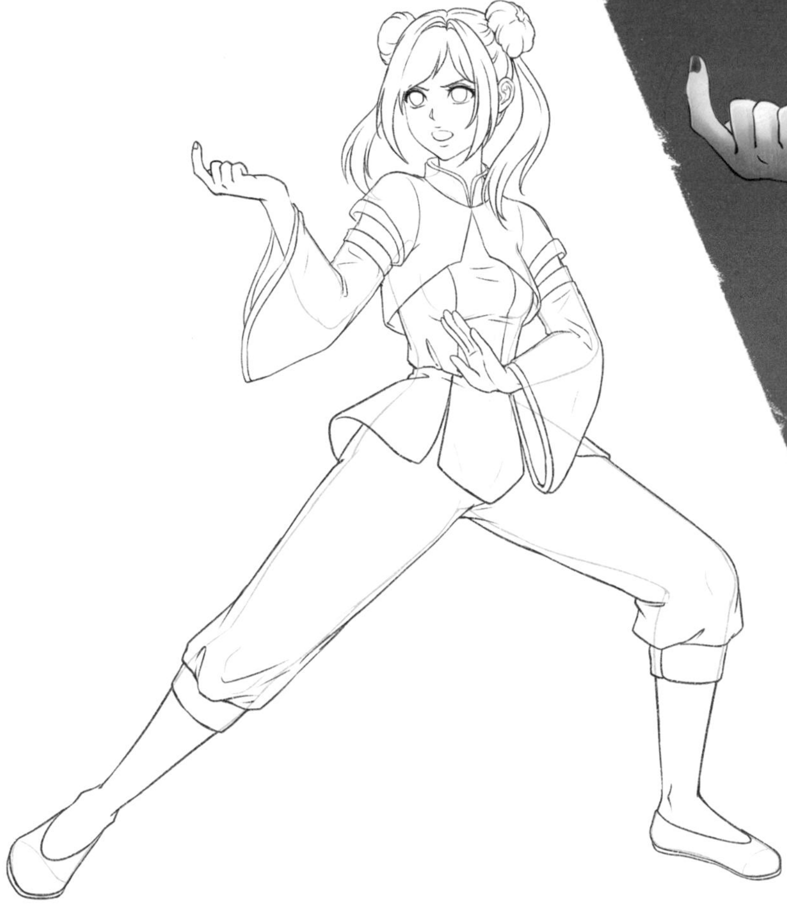

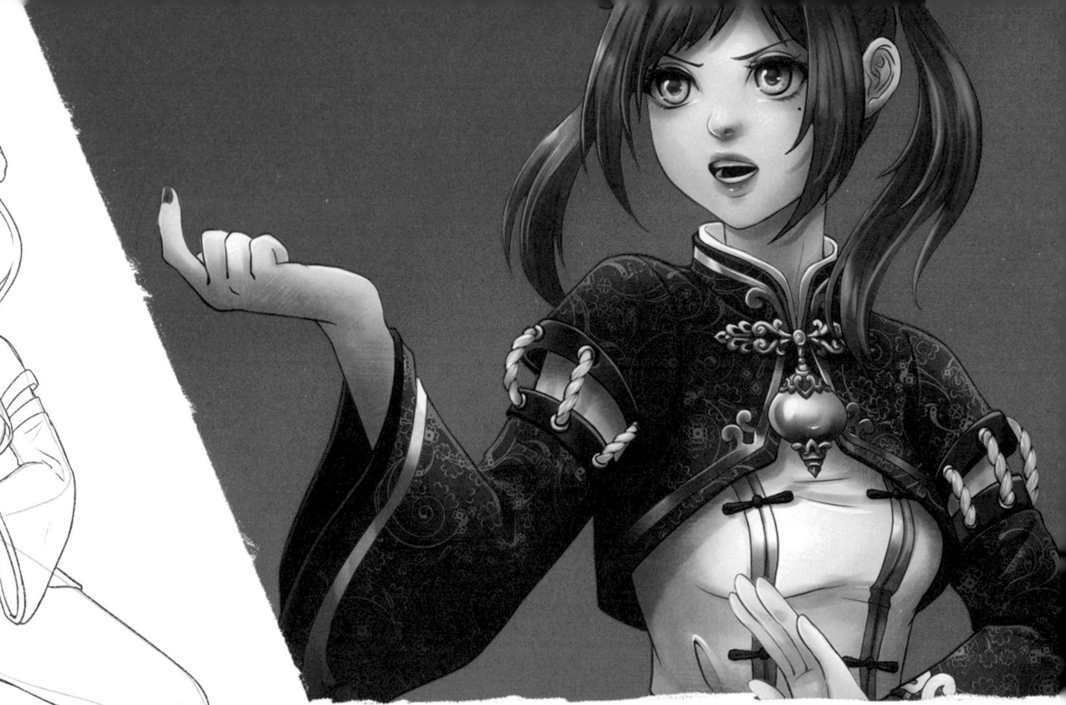

3

Martial artists' clothing tends to be loose and baggy. Design a traditional outfit, or try something more unusual. Continue adding details to the face and hair.

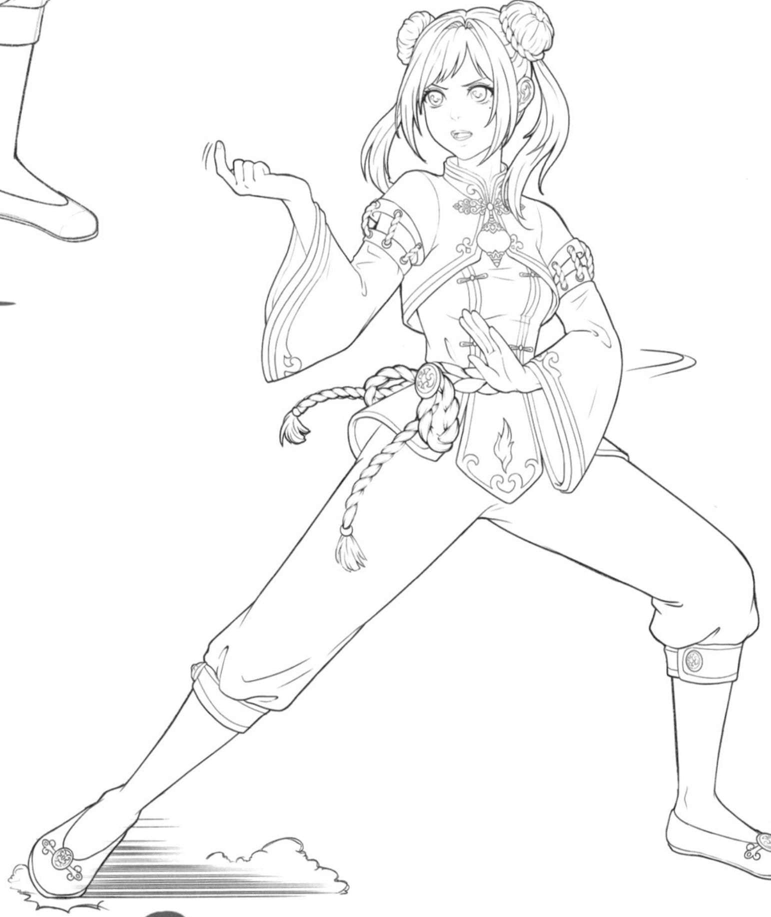

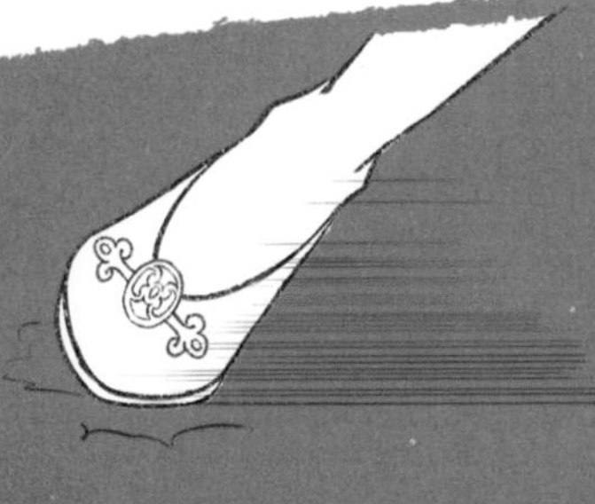

EXTRA DETAIL

'Motion blur' occurs when something is moving so quickly, it appears blurry. Motion blur extends in the opposite direction of movement, showing where the object was just a moment before.

4

Complete the face, clothes and hairstyle, detailing sections and adding shading. For the final touch, add motion blur to reveal the speed and direction of movement.

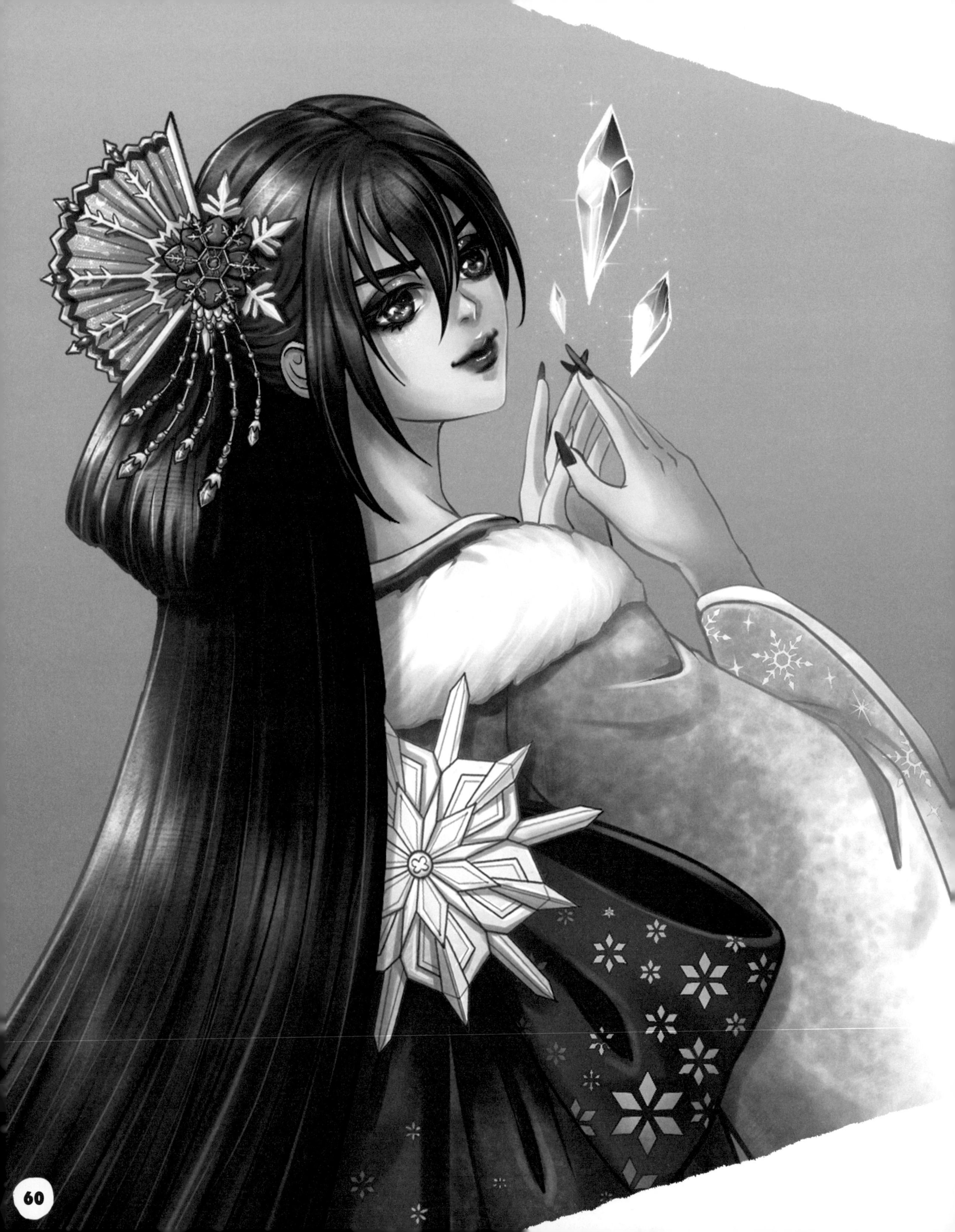

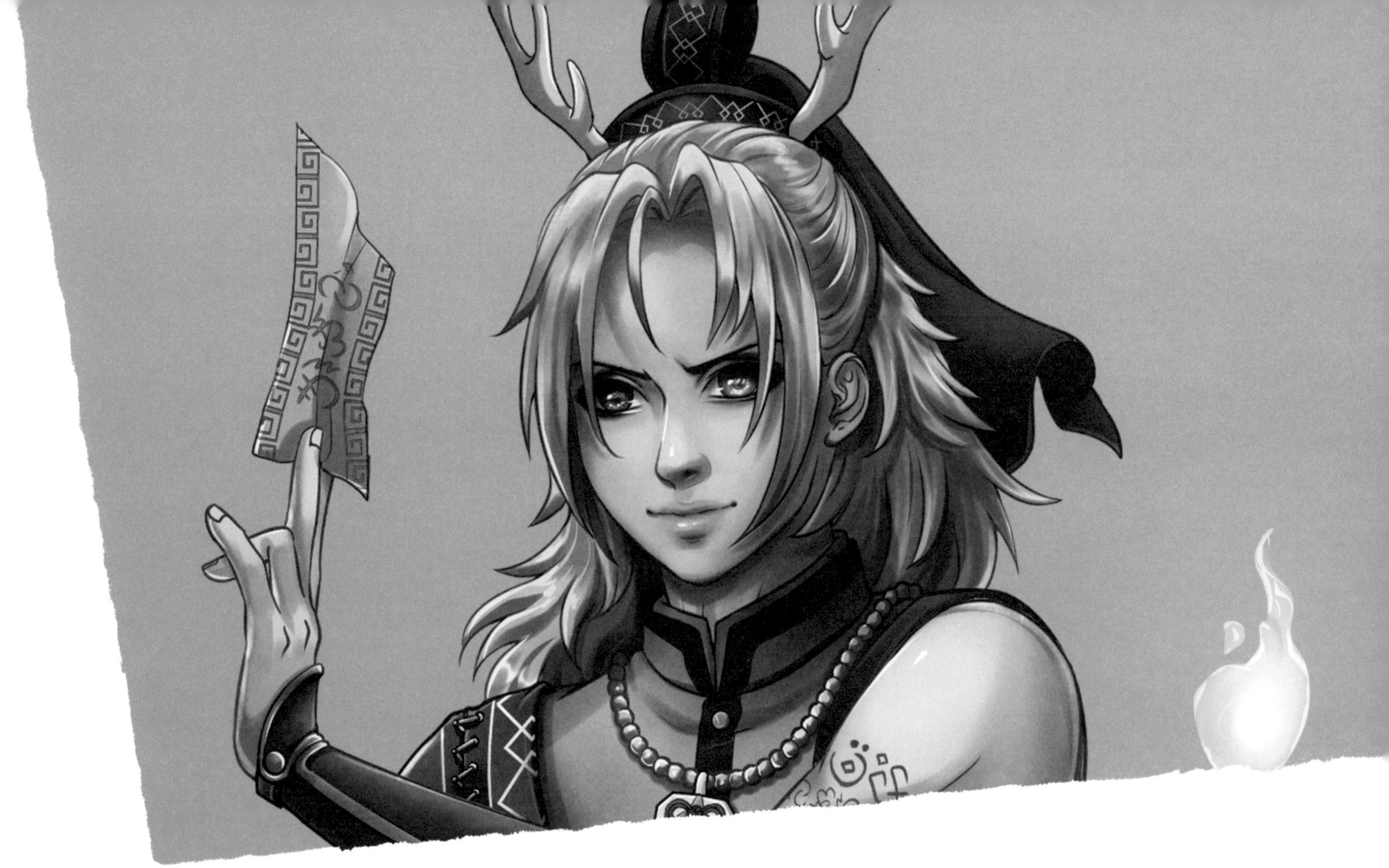

SCI-FI AND FANTASY

Venture into far-flung worlds, dystopian societies and supernatural settings with these sci-fi and fantasy characters. Create mythical creatures with supernatural powers, cyborgs with futuristic weapons, zombies, ghosts, demon slayers and more!

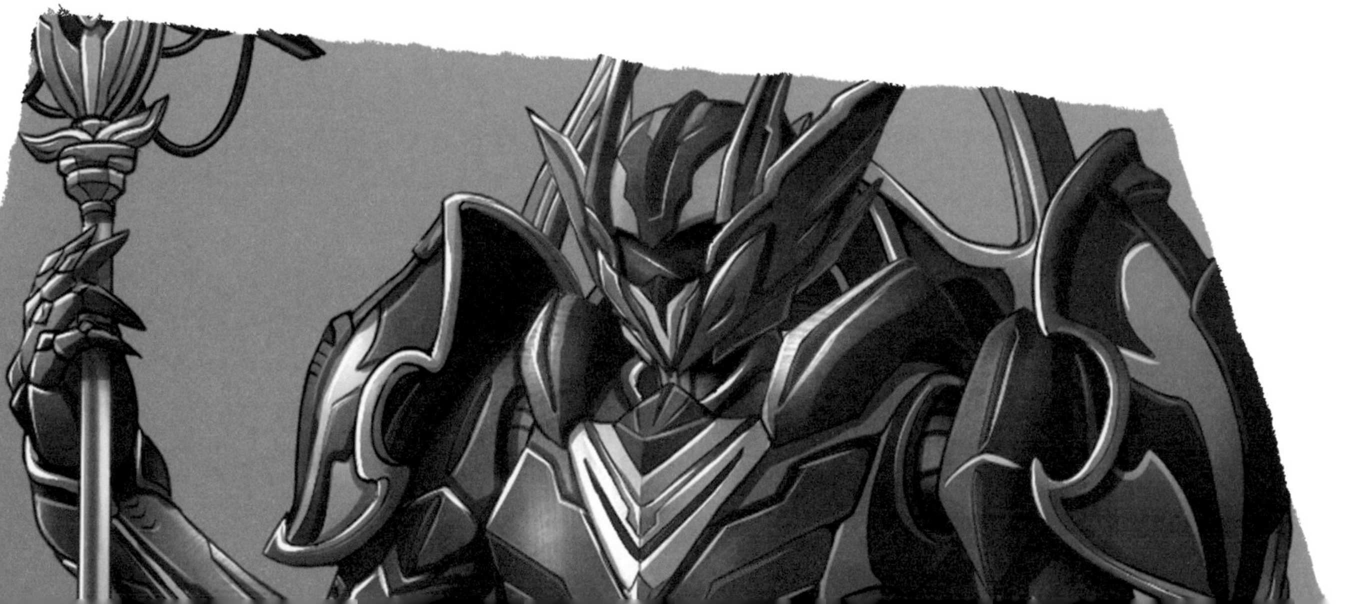

CYBERPUNK CYBORG

This futuristic cyborg character wears a high-tech costume fit for a dystopian setting. With a laser-beam weapon and communication headpiece, this cyborg is battle ready.

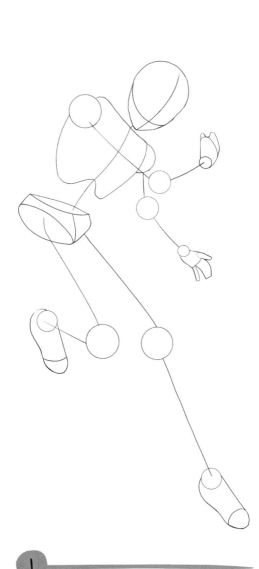

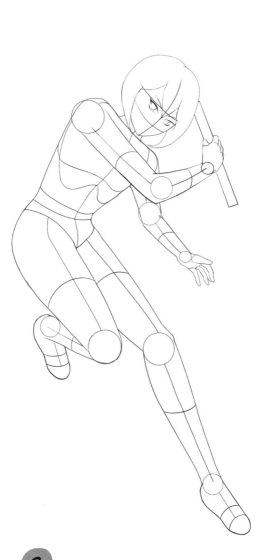

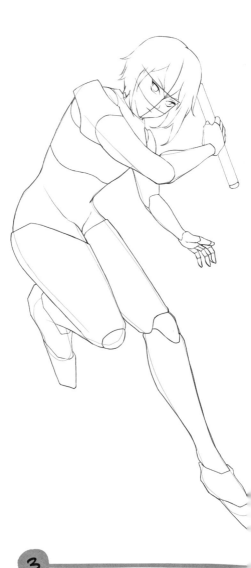

1 Start by plotting the skeleton and joints. This character is ready to defend themselves against a laser attack.

2 Sketch the figure's build, and outline the eyes and hair. Begin drawing the handle of the laser weapon.

3 Design a close-fitting, mechanical costume for your character to wear. Develop the facial features.

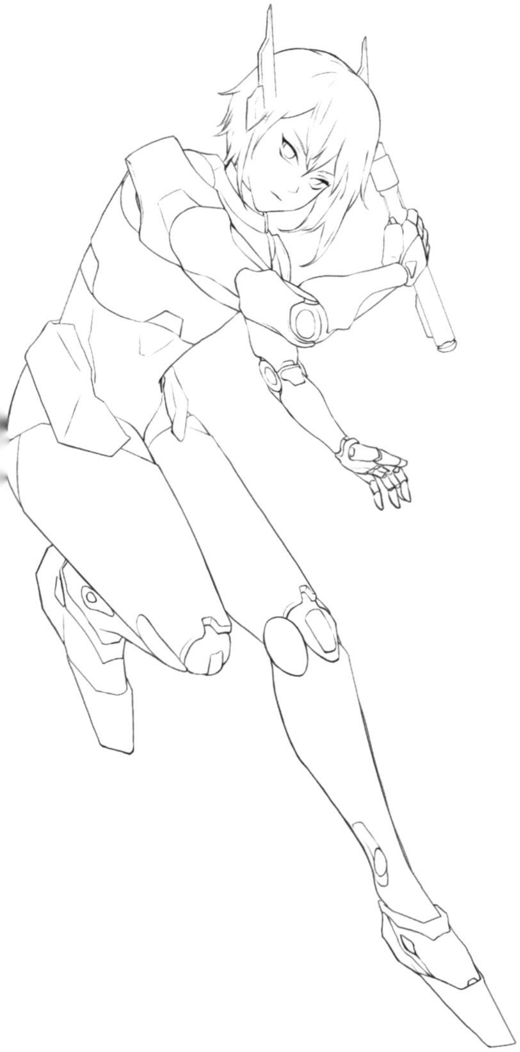

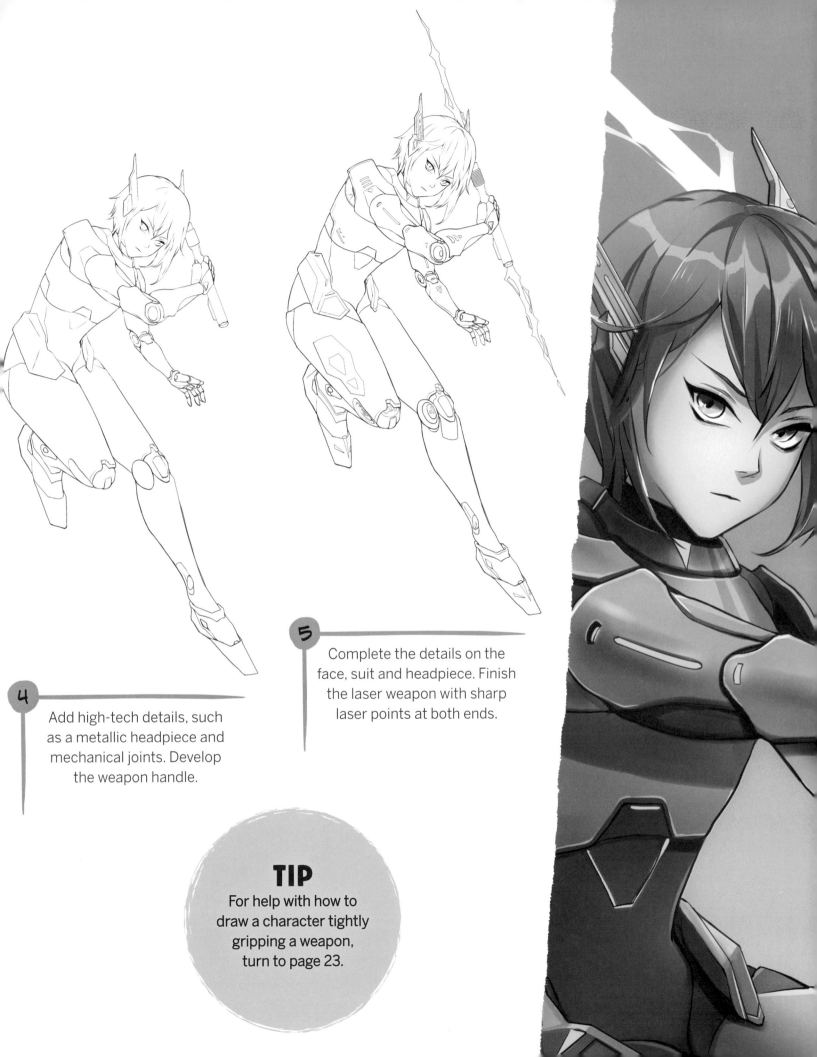

4

Add high-tech details, such as a metallic headpiece and mechanical joints. Develop the weapon handle.

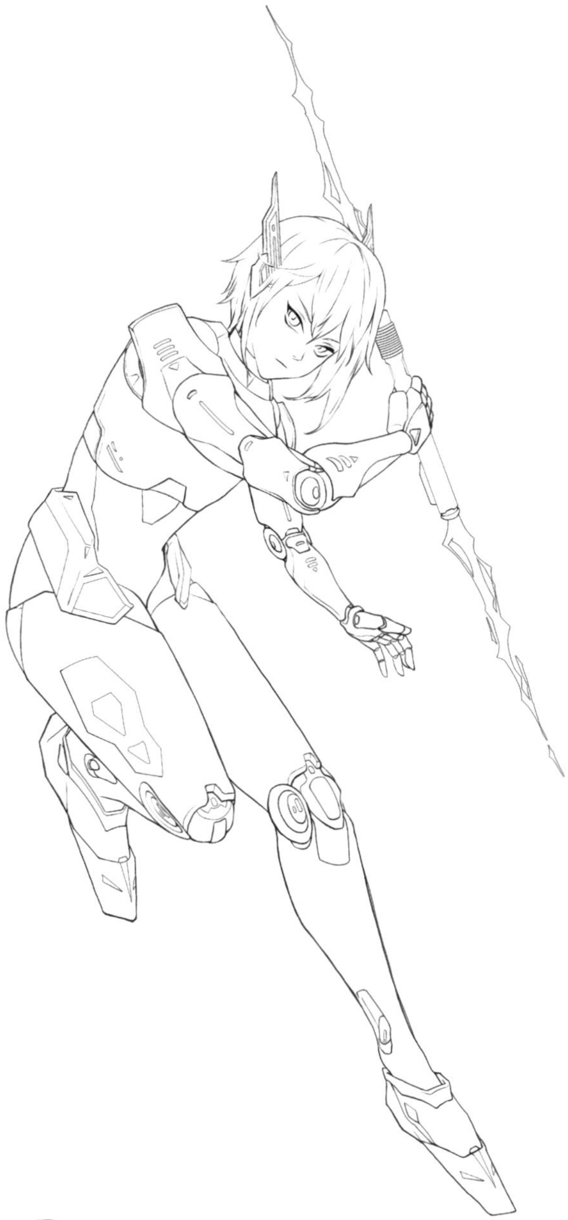

5

Complete the details on the face, suit and headpiece. Finish the laser weapon with sharp laser points at both ends.

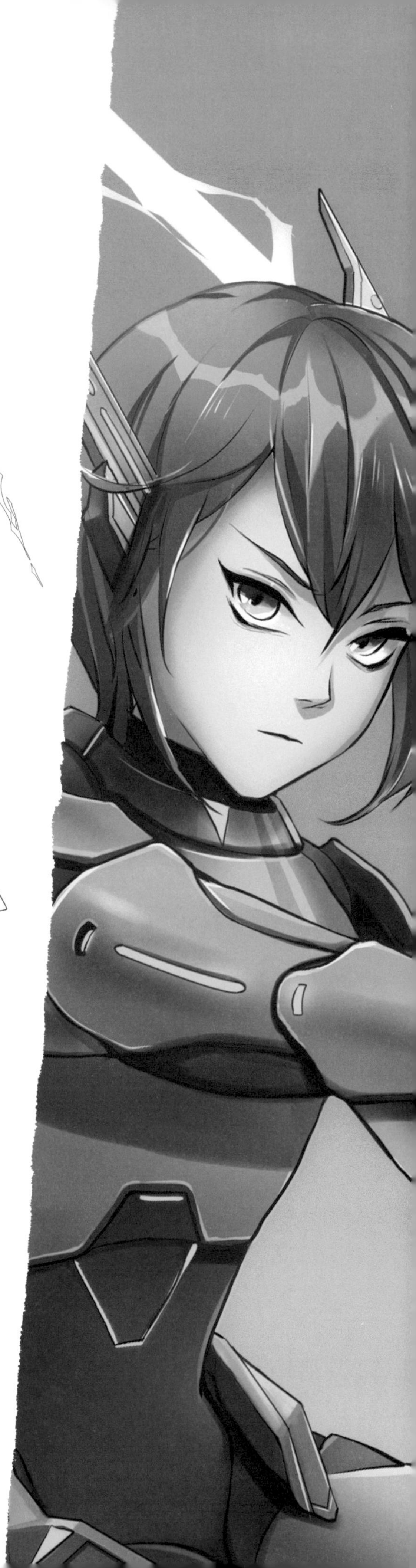

TIP

For help with how to draw a character tightly gripping a weapon, turn to page 23.

YUKI ONNA SNOW SPIRIT

Yuki Onna, or Snow Woman, is a spirit in Japanese folklore. She is described with ghostly pale skin, long black hair and striking features. In folk tales, she appears on dark snowy nights, floating gracefully above the snow.

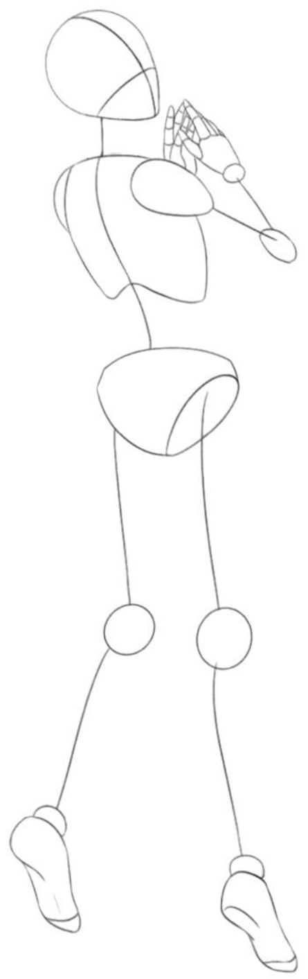

1

Sketch the skeletal structure and joints. While Yuki Onna's left arm won't be visible, consider where the arm would be, so the hand doesn't look disjointed.

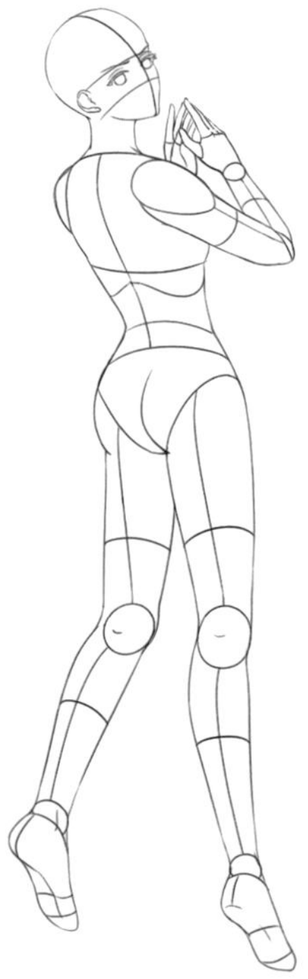

2

Flesh out Yuki Onna's build and add the eyes, bearing in mind the angle of her head (see page 11).

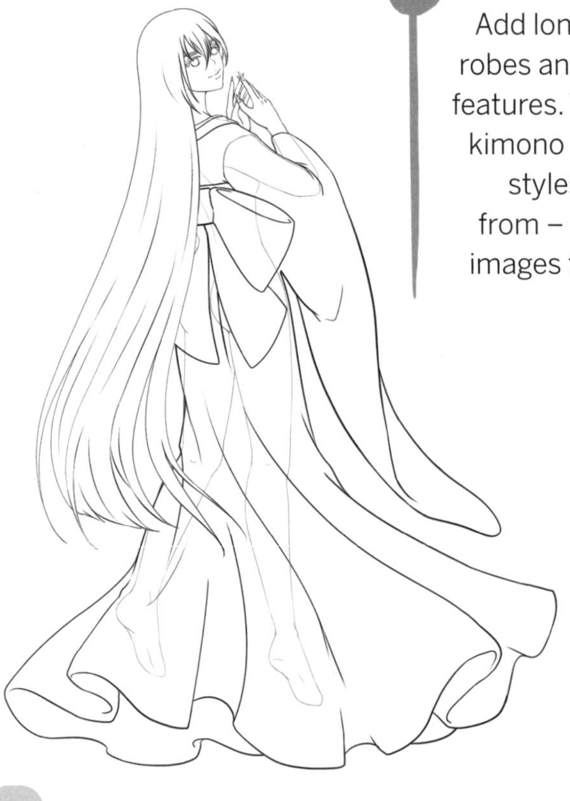

3

Add long hair, flowing robes and alluring facial features. There are many kimono and obi (sash) styles to choose from – use reference images for inspiration.

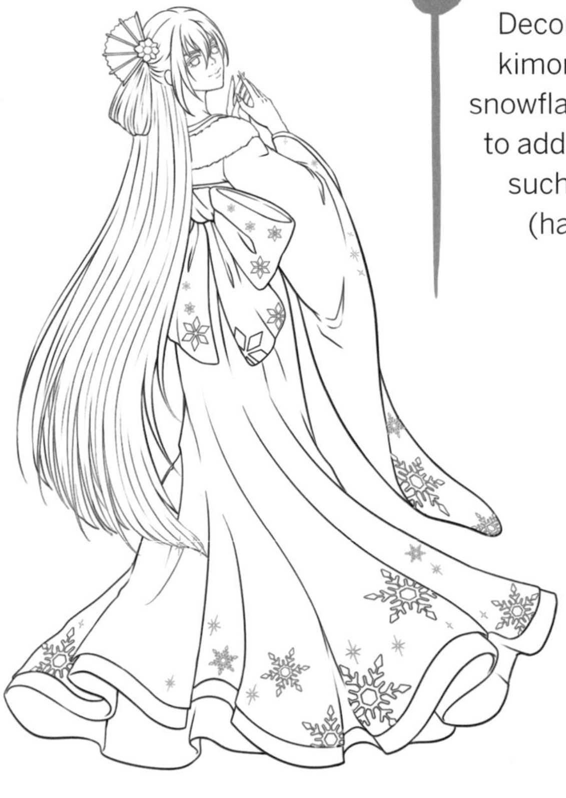

4

Decorate Yuki Onna's kimono with intricate snowflakes. You may wish to add extra decoration such as a 'kanzashi' (hair ornament).

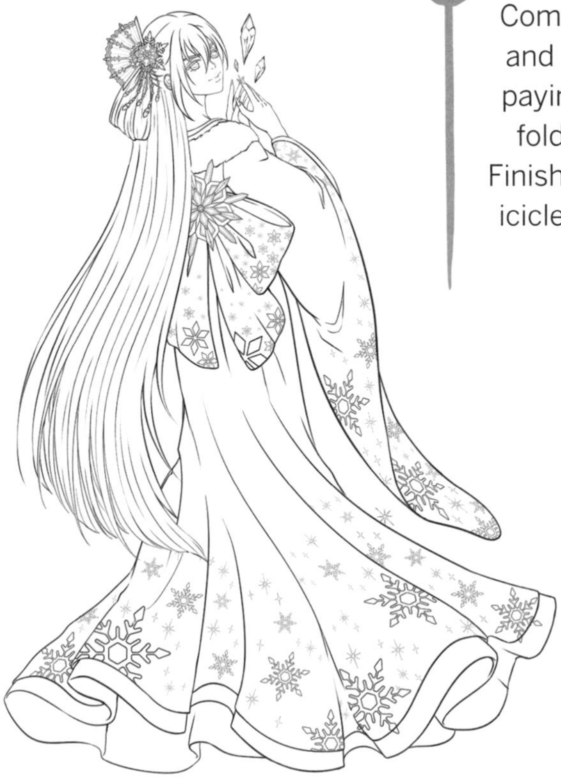

5

Complete the kanzashi and snowflake details, paying attention to the folds in the material. Finish with a few magical icicles at her fingertips.

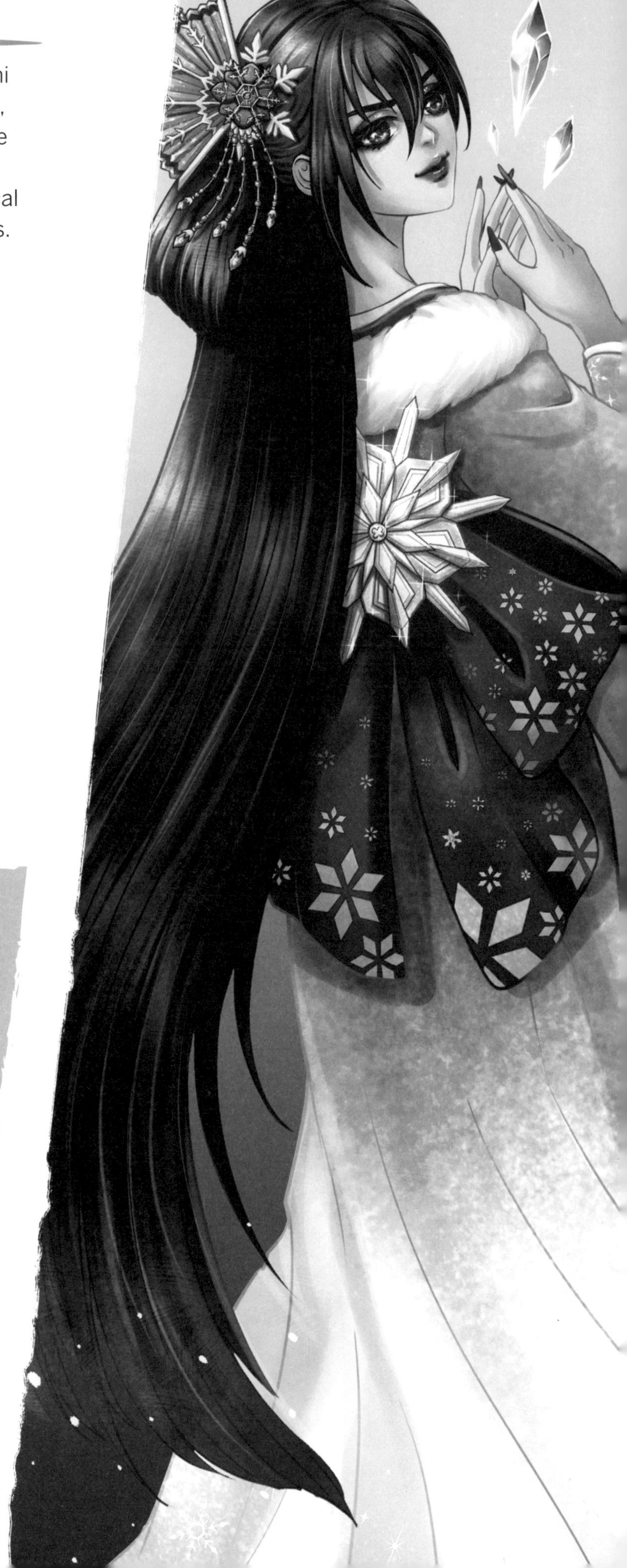

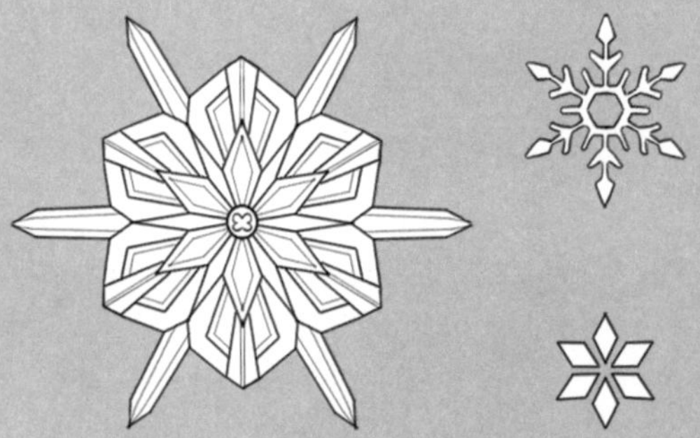

EXTRA DETAIL

To draw a snowflake, start at the middle and work your way outwards, adding shapes such as diamonds, triangles and oblongs. Keep shapes sharp rather than rounded and ensure your snowflakes are symmetrical.

ZOMBIE

With a hollow figure, ripped clothes and haunting face, this gruesome zombie is ready to hunt for its living victims. This character is all about the details!

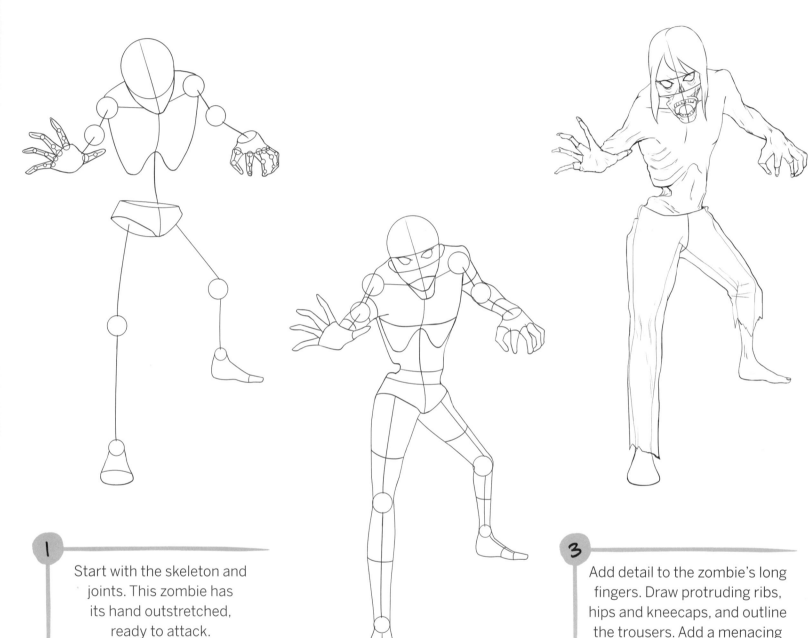

1 Start with the skeleton and joints. This zombie has its hand outstretched, ready to attack.

2 Determine your character's build. It may be hunched over, with thin, sinewy arms and a wasted torso. Outline the eyes.

3 Add detail to the zombie's long fingers. Draw protruding ribs, hips and kneecaps, and outline the trousers. Add a menacing expression, with a gaping mouth.

EXTRA DETAIL

Dress your zombie in rags – start by outlining complete clothes, then draw jagged rips in the material and show the torso underneath. Keep the edges rough and frayed.

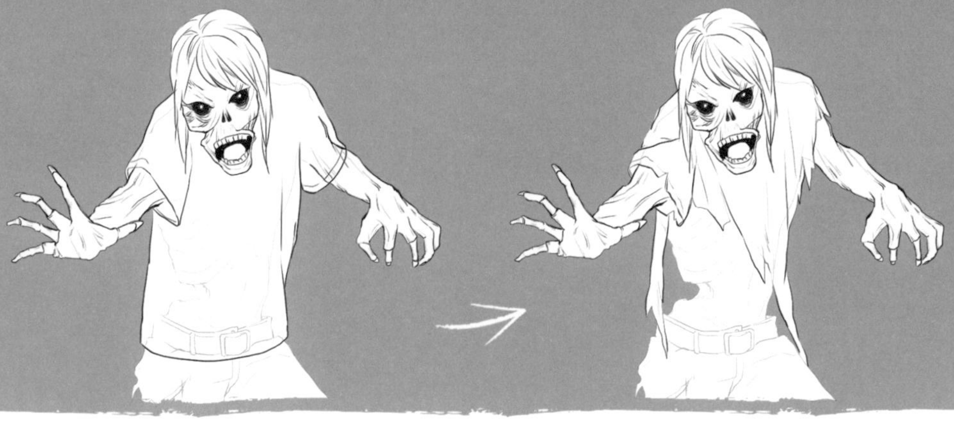

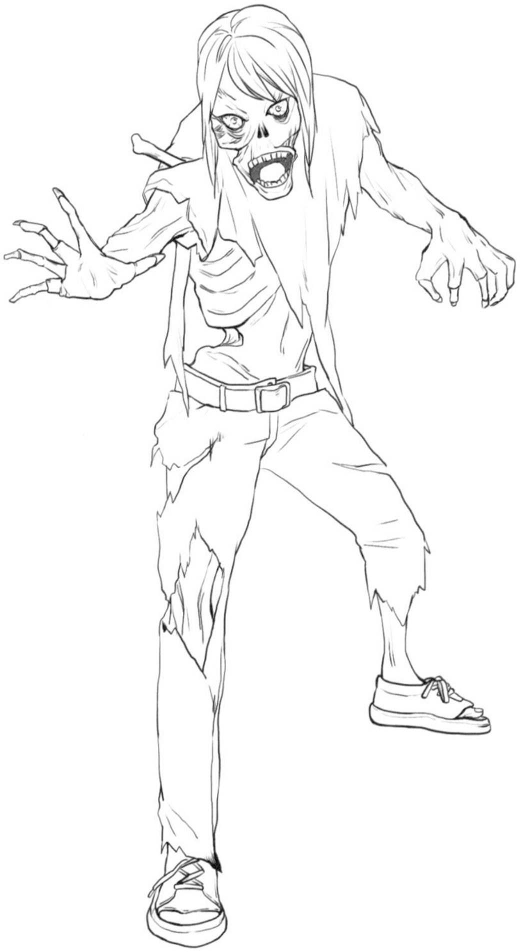

4

Draw the zombie's clothes and shoes, making them look torn and rotting to show that they are decaying. Finish off its facial features and hair.

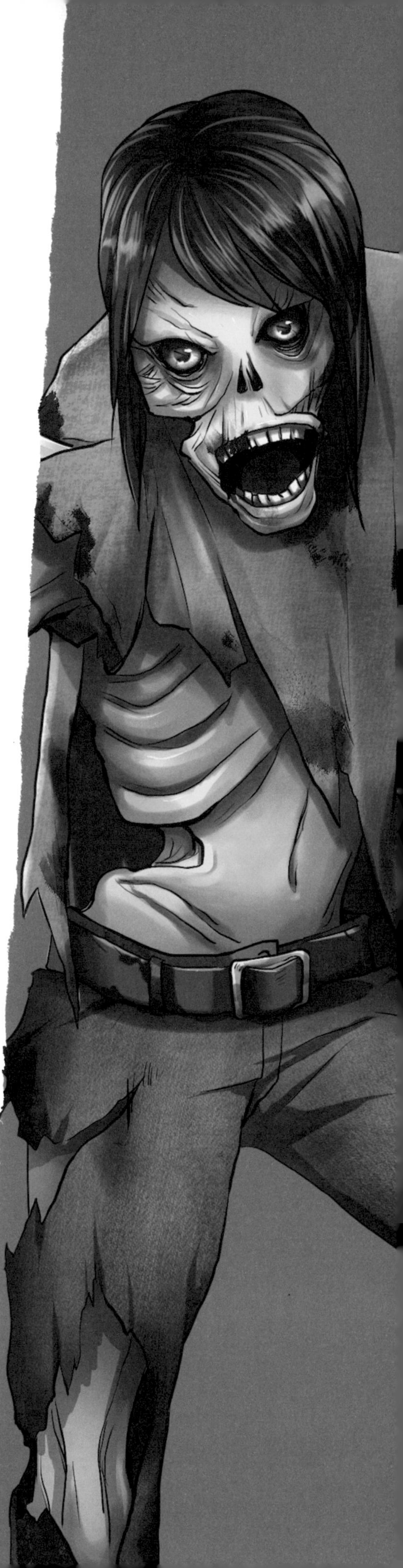

VAMPIRE KNIGHT

This sword-wielding knight is as brave as he is impeccably dressed.
When you've finished drawing him, he'll be the talk of the realm.

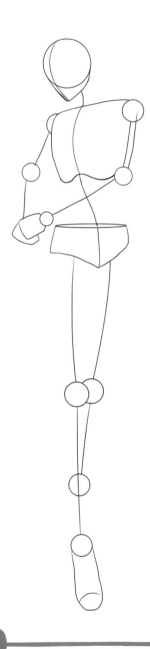

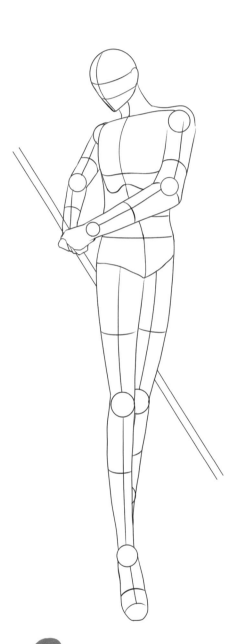

1 Sketch the basic skeleton and joints. This knight is leaning to one side, as if about to draw his sword.

2 Flesh out a tall, lean body shape, using the guidelines. Sketch the outline of a sword crossing behind his body.

3 Outline the hair, eyes and a sophisticated outfit, including a cape draped over the shoulder. Add a basic sword shape.

TIP

You may wish to go over the final lines with fineliner pens. Experiment with using fine tips for detail and thicker nibs for outlines.

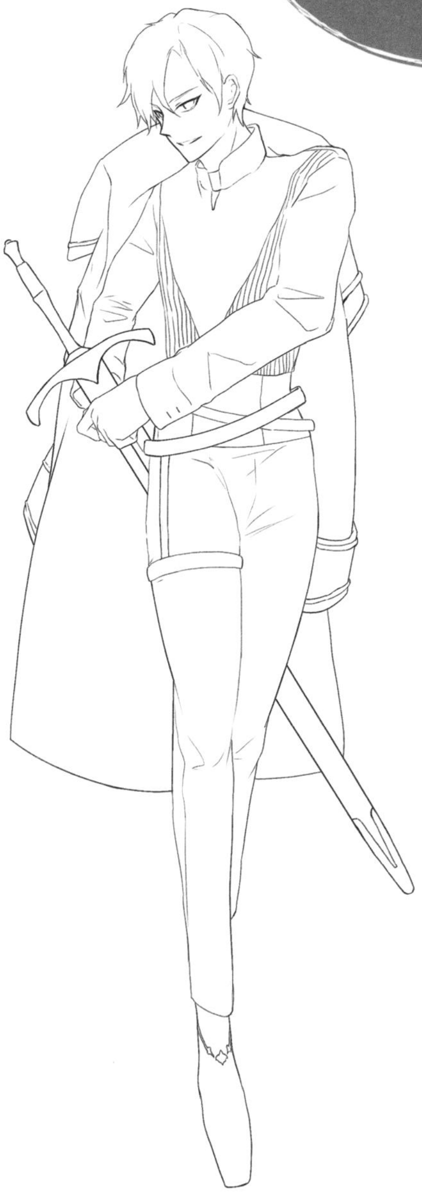

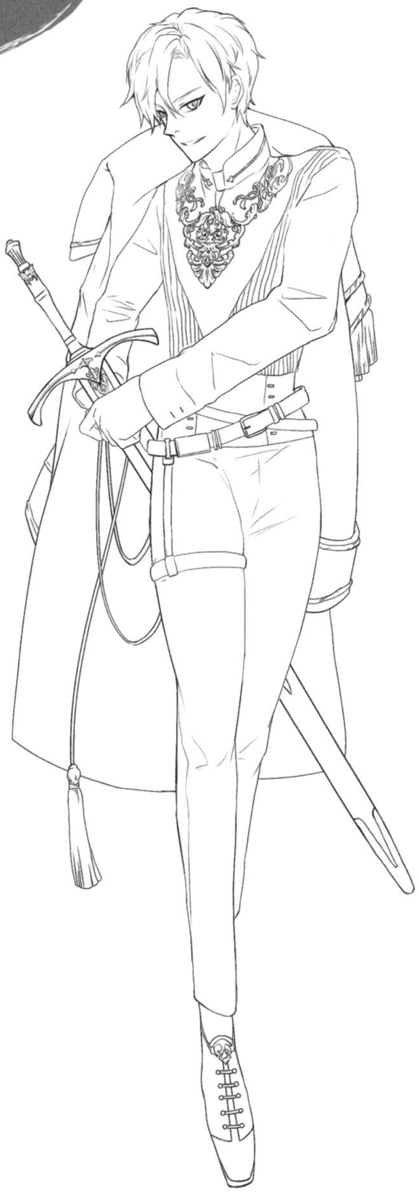

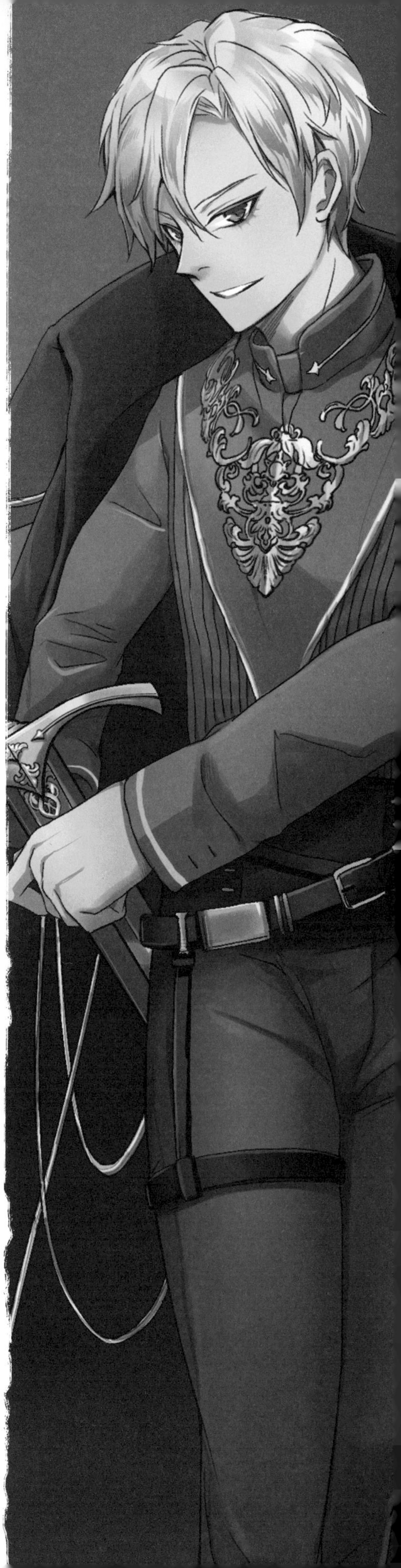

4

Further develop the face, hair, weapon and clothes. A floppy hairstyle may suit his nonchalant attitude.

5

Continue adding details. The decorated waistcoat and intricate embroidery on the knight's shirt lend character.

MECHA ROBOT

A mecha is a giant robot or machine. It can be any size and style, but is usually much larger – and stronger – than a human. Give this formidable creation a go!

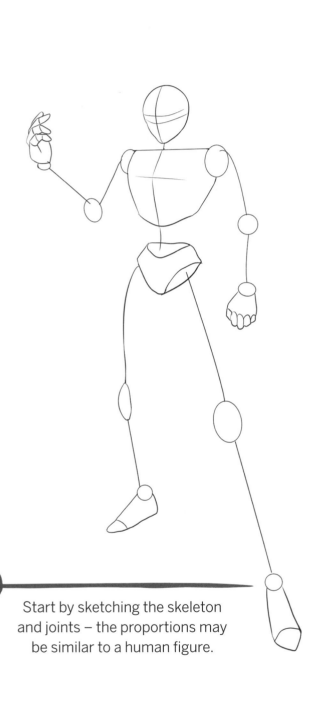

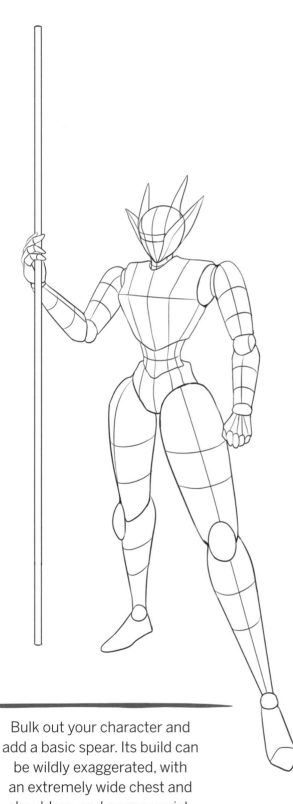

1 Start by sketching the skeleton and joints – the proportions may be similar to a human figure.

2 Bulk out your character and add a basic spear. Its build can be wildly exaggerated, with an extremely wide chest and shoulders, and narrow waist.

TIP
Made of super-strong metal, your mecha should look solid and indestructible. A shiny, metallic surface will add to the effect.

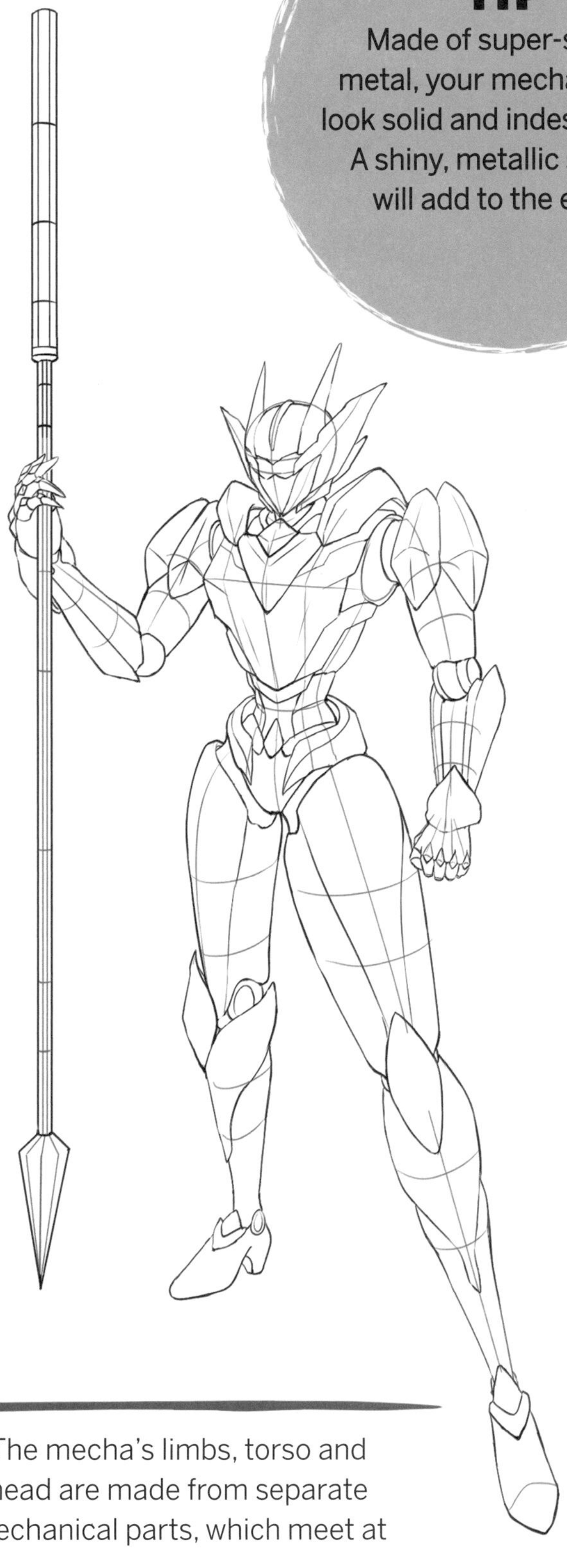

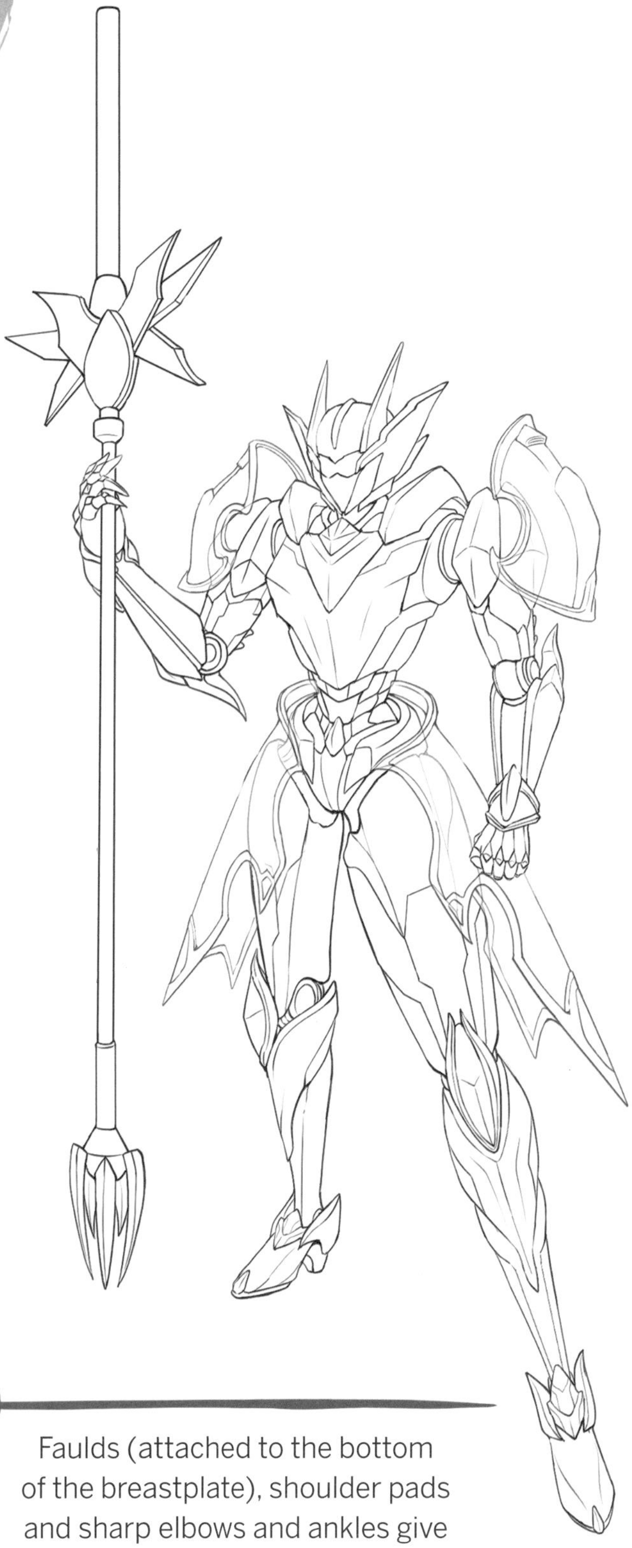

3

The mecha's limbs, torso and head are made from separate mechanical parts, which meet at joints. Start adding details to the armour and develop the spear.

4

Faulds (attached to the bottom of the breastplate), shoulder pads and sharp elbows and ankles give your character a daunting look.

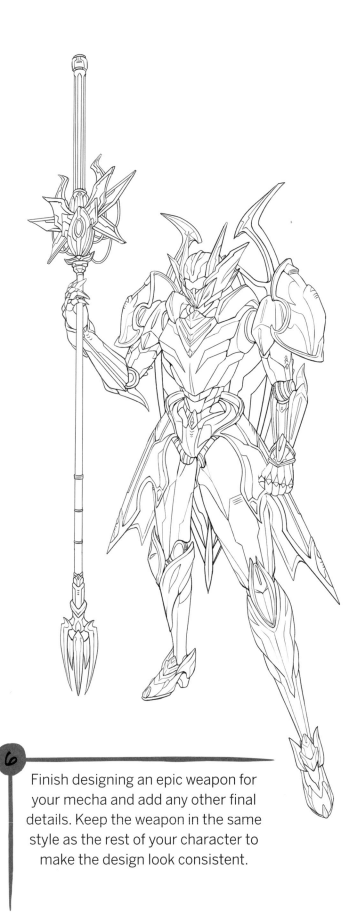

6

Finish designing an epic weapon for your mecha and add any other final details. Keep the weapon in the same style as the rest of your character to make the design look consistent.

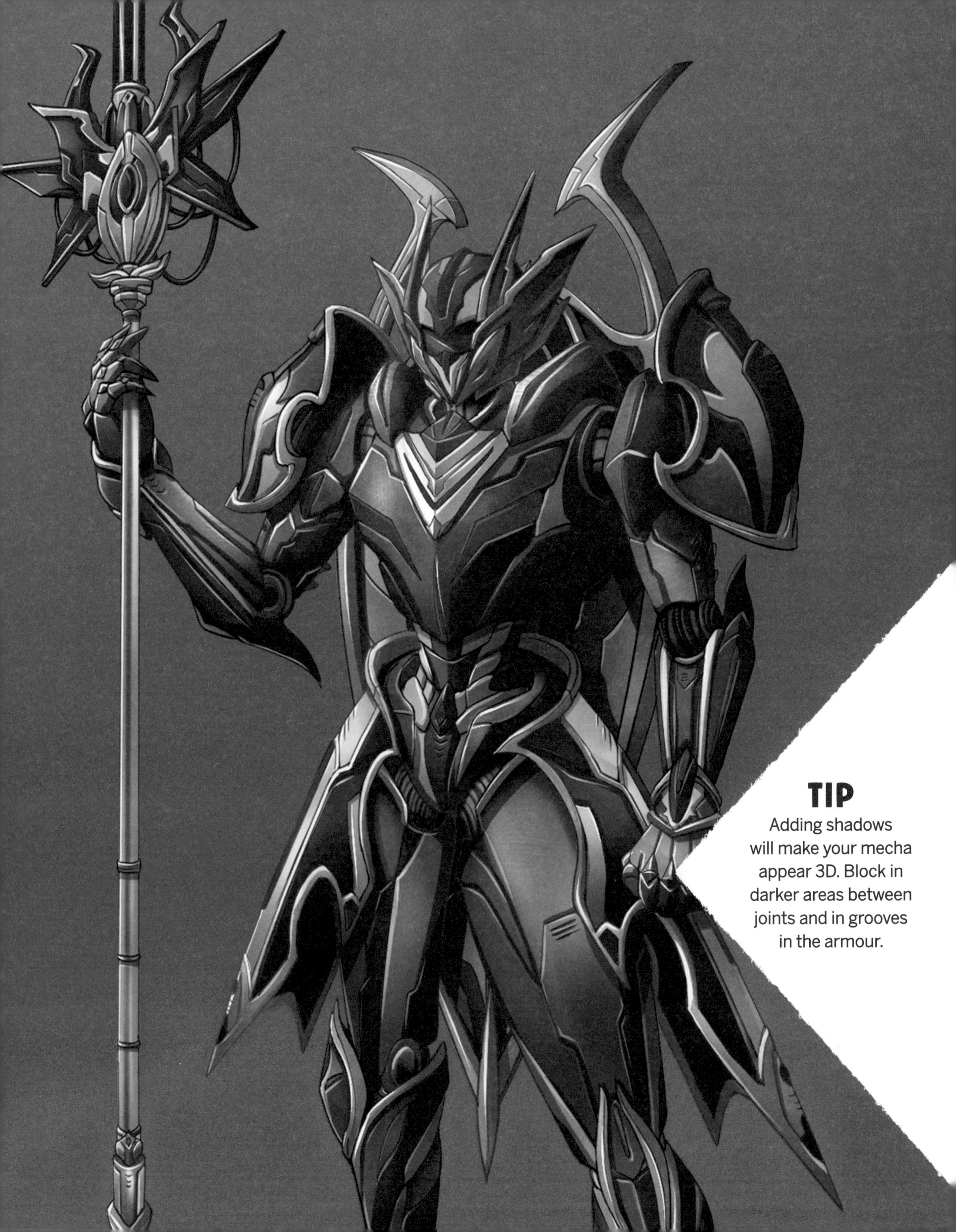

TIP

Adding shadows will make your mecha appear 3D. Block in darker areas between joints and in grooves in the armour.

GHOST PRINCESS

The mash-up of creepy and cute is a popular manga theme. This ghost princess is drawn with an enlarged head and eyes for extra cuteness.

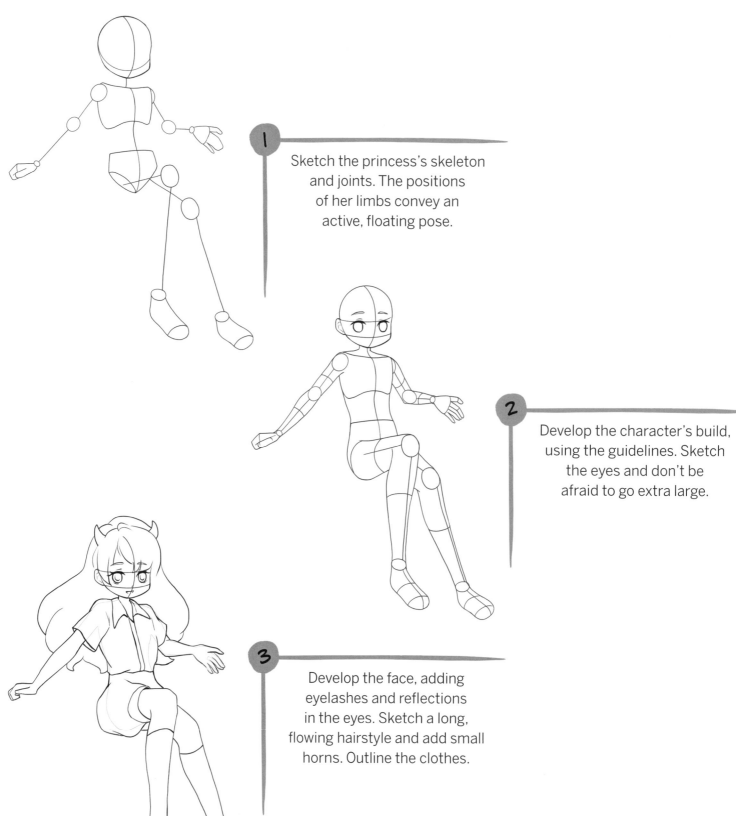

1 Sketch the princess's skeleton and joints. The positions of her limbs convey an active, floating pose.

2 Develop the character's build, using the guidelines. Sketch the eyes and don't be afraid to go extra large.

3 Develop the face, adding eyelashes and reflections in the eyes. Sketch a long, flowing hairstyle and add small horns. Outline the clothes.

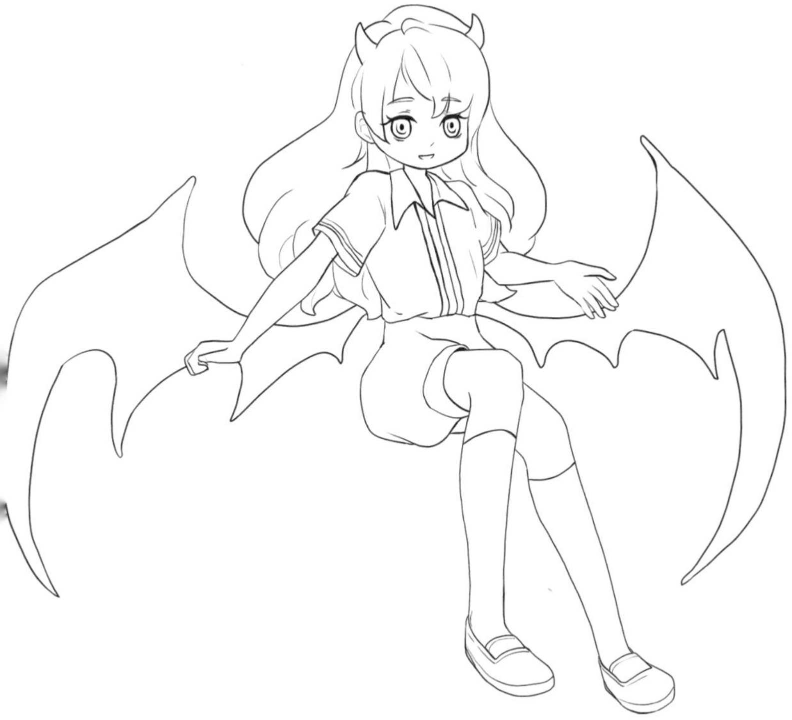

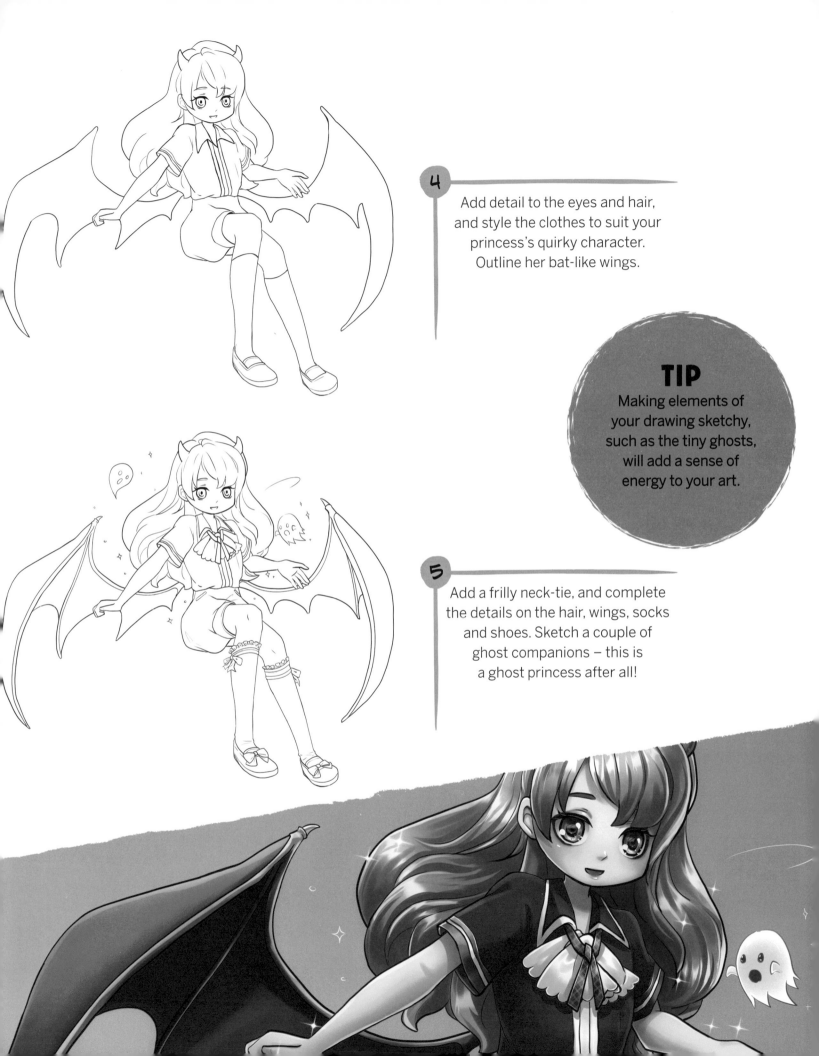

4

Add detail to the eyes and hair, and style the clothes to suit your princess's quirky character. Outline her bat-like wings.

TIP

Making elements of your drawing sketchy, such as the tiny ghosts, will add a sense of energy to your art.

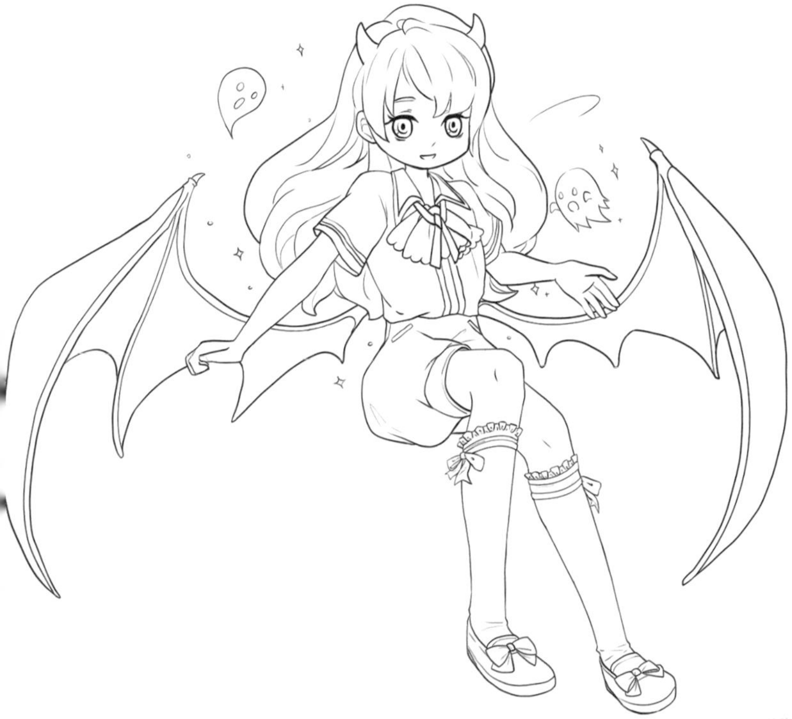

5

Add a frilly neck-tie, and complete the details on the hair, wings, socks and shoes. Sketch a couple of ghost companions – this is a ghost princess after all!

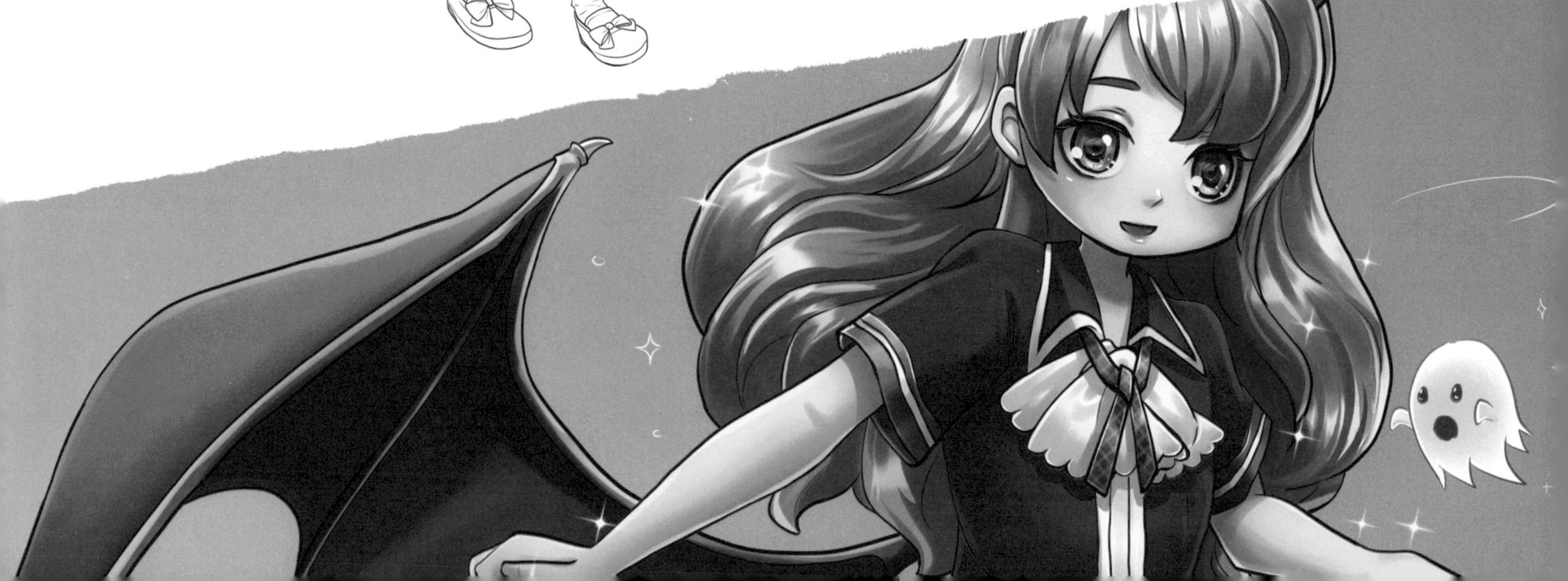

DEMON SLAYER

Demon slayers are incredible warriors who may specialize in combat, martial arts or magic. This character is using charms and talismans, revealing his magical abilities.

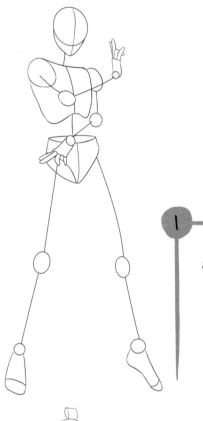

1 Consider what special abilities your character may have and design the pose accordingly, starting with the skeleton and joints.

2 Develop your character's build. Outline the hair and the two paper amulets that they're holding.

3 Sketch the base clothing, keeping the silhouette simple before adding more details. Add the eyes, and draw floating amulets and talismans around him.

TIP
Would your demon slayer suit a tattoo? Decorate him as much as you wish, using tattoo designs and patterns to spark ideas.

TIP

You could use numbers, letters and symbols to decorate your paper amulets, making them look mysterious.

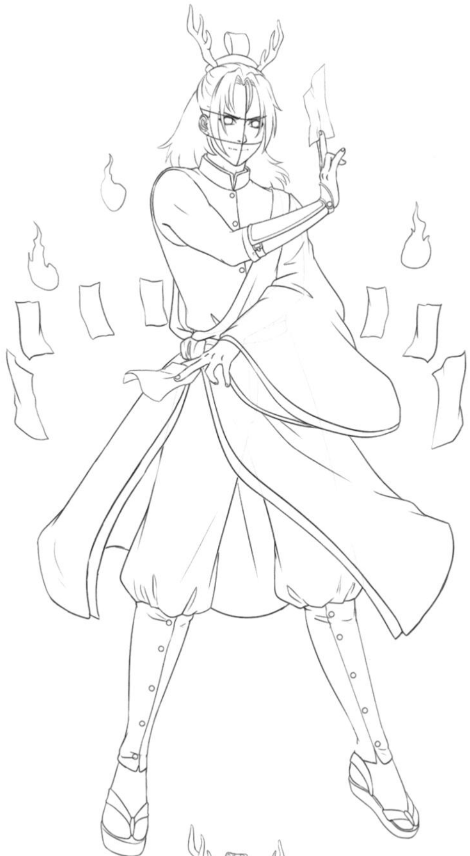

4

Develop the face and clothing, adding swishing robes and a headpiece. This character's headpiece contains elements of a Shinto priest's headwear and the horns of a kirin (a mythical hoofed creature).

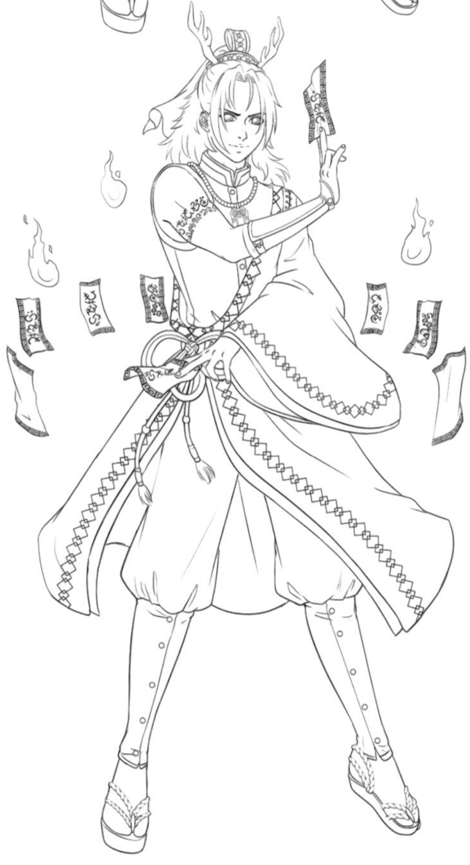

5

Finish by adding jewellery and charms. Draw details on the paper amulets and add stitching to the cloak. Complete the facial features and eyes.

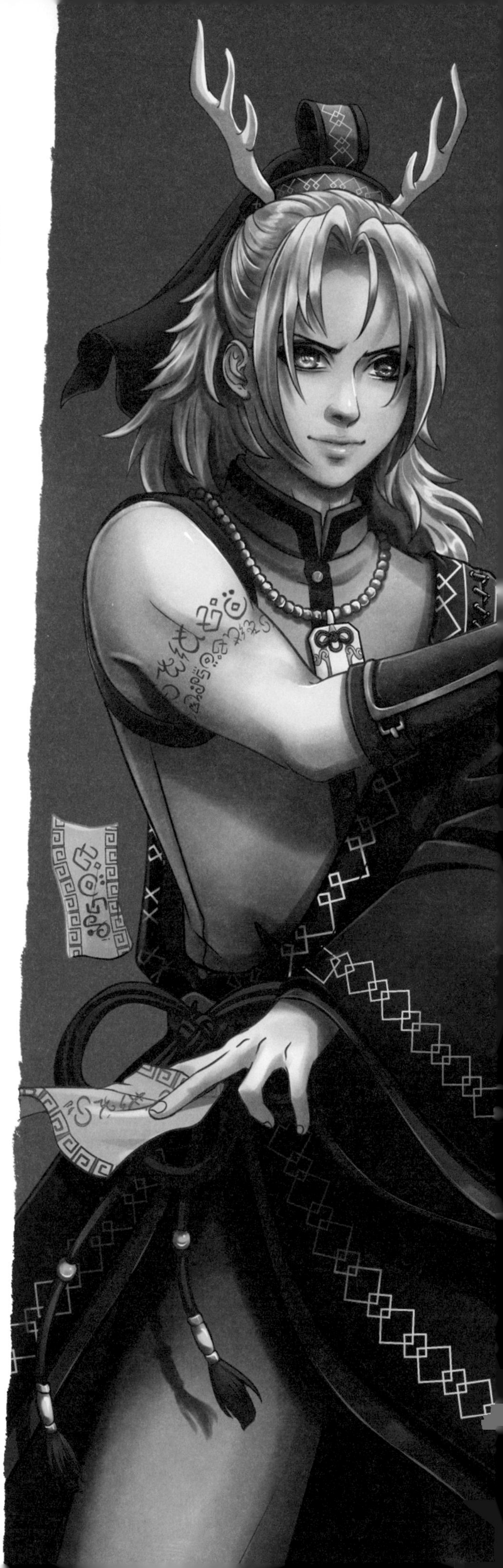

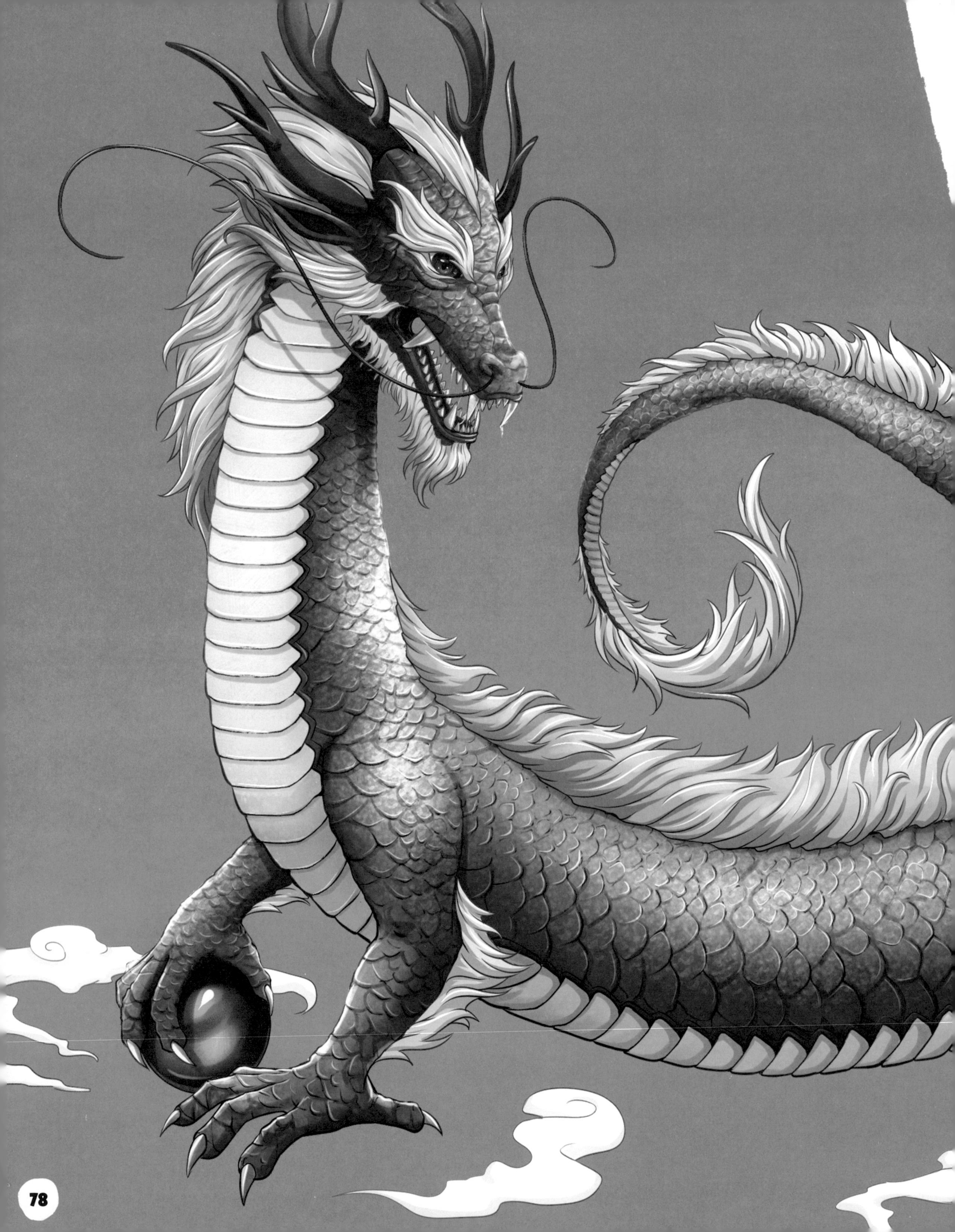

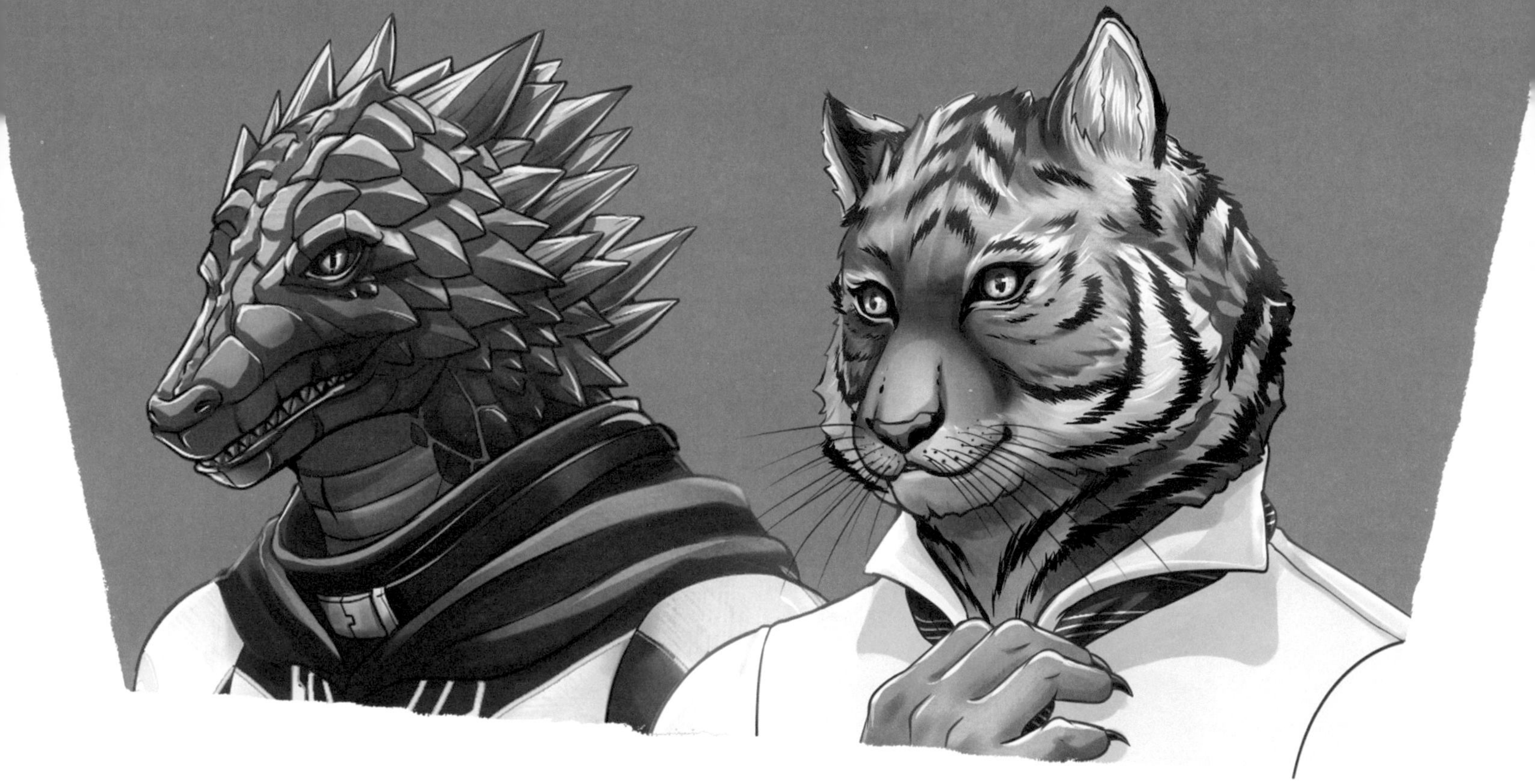

MONSTERS, ANIMALS AND ANTHROS

Explore the weird, the wild and the grisly in this final chapter. Discover the differences between human and animal anatomy, and design folklore creatures, dragons and anthropomorphic creations. Take your drawings one step further by thinking about backgrounds for your characters, too.

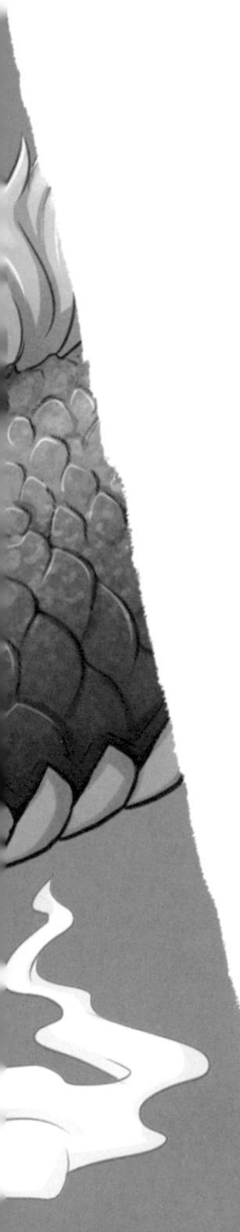

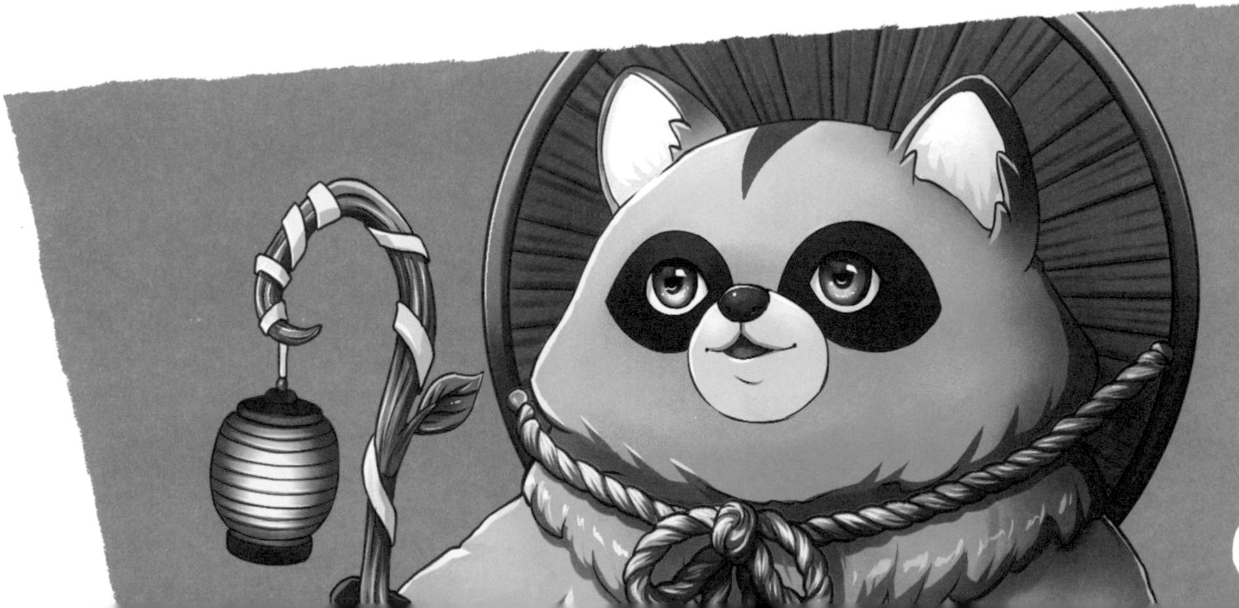

TANUKI AND KITSUNE

The Tanuki and Kitsune are creatures from Japanese folklore likely to capture hearts. The Kitsune is fox-like, with five or nine tails, and thought to be rather sly, while Tanuki is based on the Japanese raccoon dog and is considered cheeky and jolly.

TANUKI

1

This Tanuki is bipedal (it walks on two legs). Its body is egg-shaped and the head looks like a squashed circle. Sketch the ears, limbs and tail.

2

Build your character's form. Think of the body as a 3D sphere rather than a 2D shape. Keep the guidelines curved so the Tanuki's figure looks full. Add a staff, sake jar and iconic turtle-shell hat.

3

Add details to the staff and sake jar. Develop the body with tufts of fur and little paws. Add details to the face.

4

Give your Tanuki some patterns around the eyes, belly, tail and forehead and complete the details on the hat, jar and staff.

1 Kitsunes, like foxes, are quadrupedal – they walk on four legs. The face is diamond-shaped with pointy ears and the body is rounded, as shown.

2 Develop your character's rounded, sprightly shape. Keep the guidelines curved to give the drawing depth. Sketch the eyes, ears, paws and nine tails.

3 Add details to the face and tufts of fur around the ears and neck. In some legends, the Kitsune wears a necklace associated with the 13 elements of Japanese mythology.

4 Finish by adding patterns to the fur on the Kitsune's forehead. Add detail to the tips of the ears and the tails.

WEREWOLF

Legend tells us that werewolves are humans who transform into fearsome wolves on the full Moon. Reference images of wolves may help with the anatomy of the head.

1 First, plot the skeleton and joints. This werewolf is hunched and snarling from the physical exertion of its transformation.

TIP
Why not add a background with a full Moon shining over a forest of dark trees to enhance the eerie effect?

2 This character has a robust, muscular build, with the head of a wolf and arms, legs and torso similar to a human. Its feet and hands are long and clawed.

3

Develop the facial features and give it a vicious expression. Add tufts of fur around the ears, head and tail. Short fur on the body reveals its muscular frame. Start to add cracks on the ground.

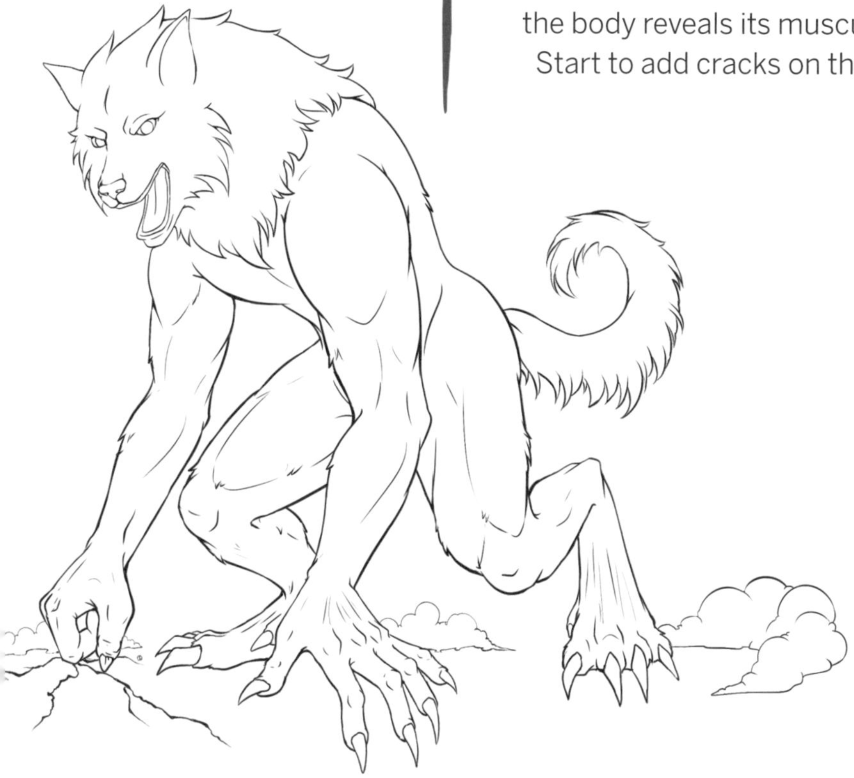

4

Add eyebrows, whiskers and teeth, and dress your werewolf in ripped clothes. Special effects, such as cracks in the ground and a large cloud of dust, enhance the drama.

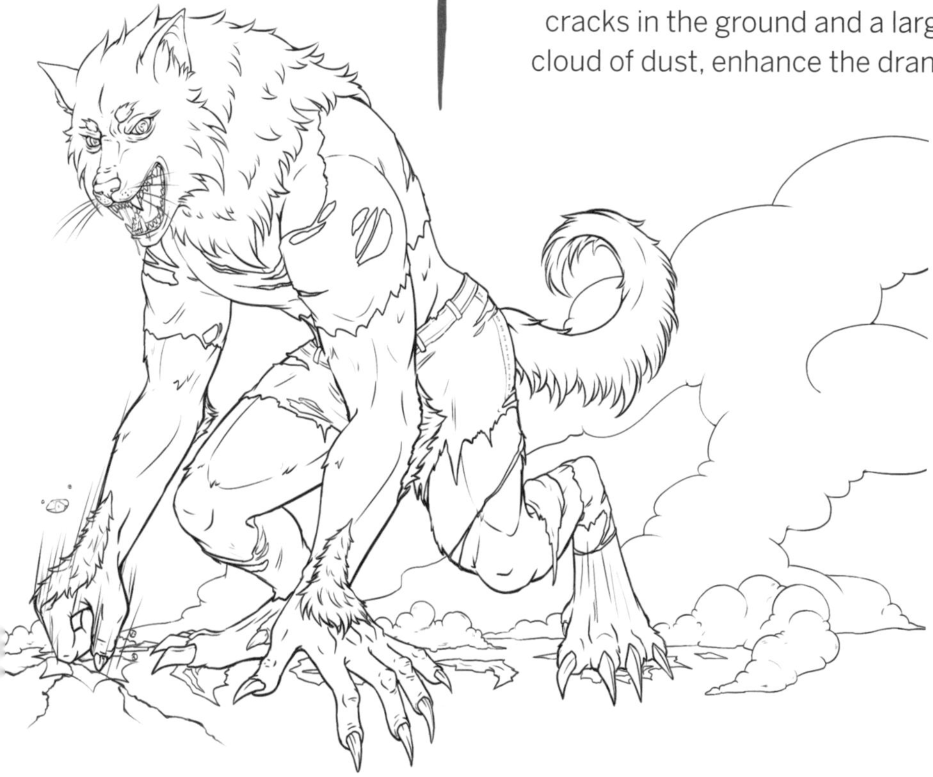

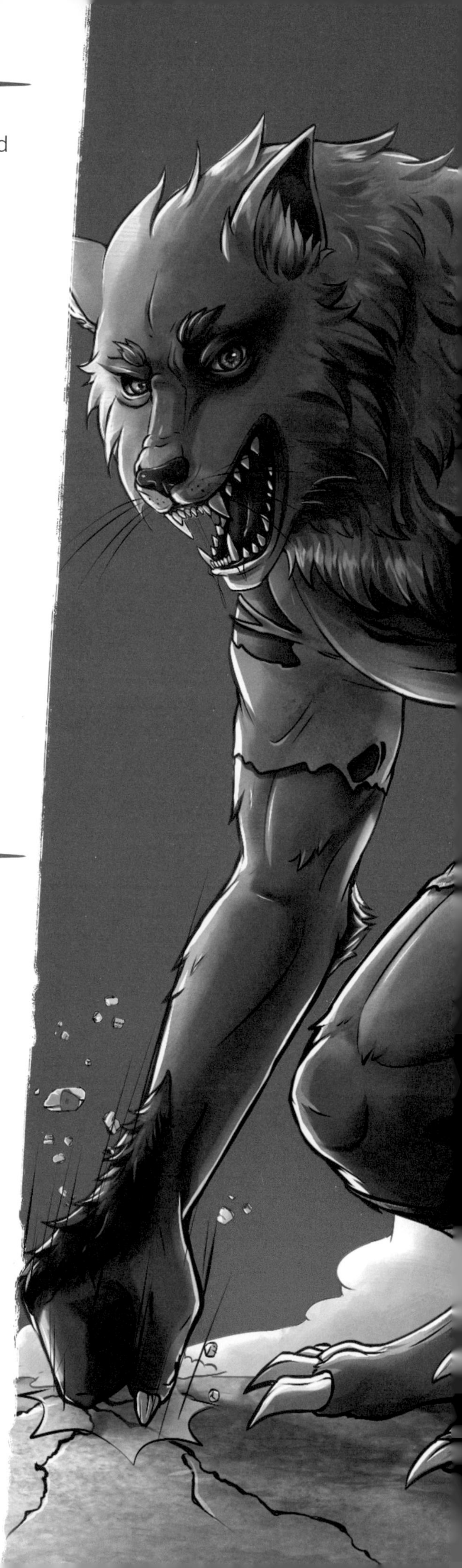

EASTERN DRAGON

Eastern dragons are regarded as symbols of good fortune and strength. Unlike Western dragons, they have long, serpentine bodies and can fly, but are not depicted with wings. This dragon carries a pearl in its claw, which symbolizes wisdom.

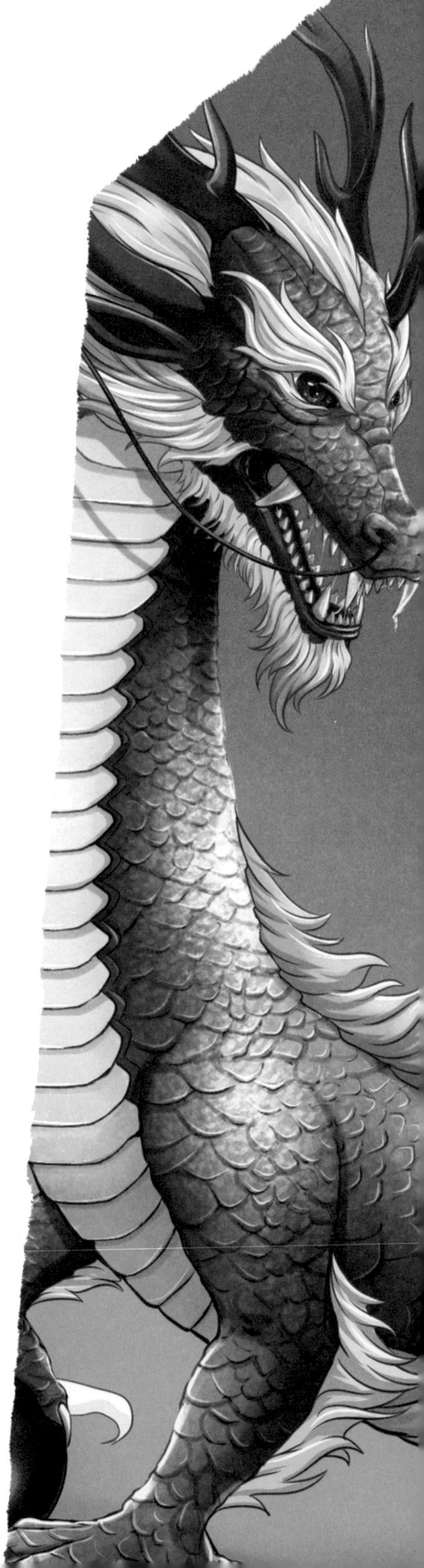

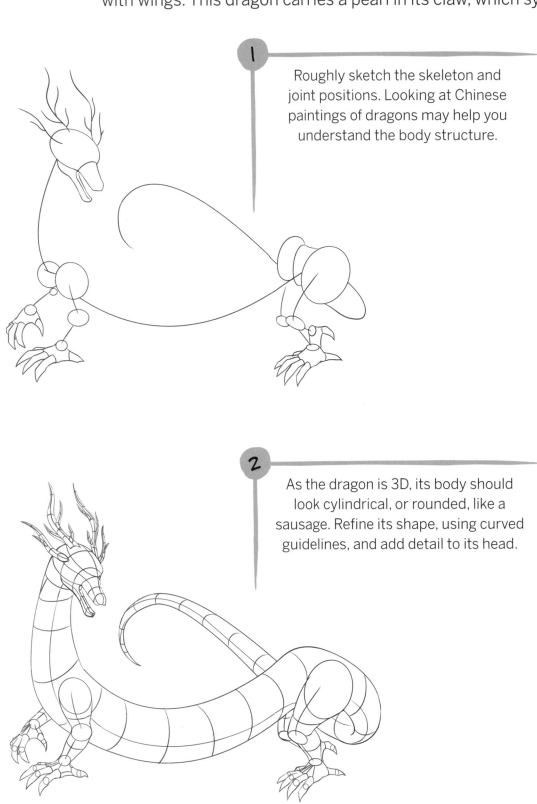

1

Roughly sketch the skeleton and joint positions. Looking at Chinese paintings of dragons may help you understand the body structure.

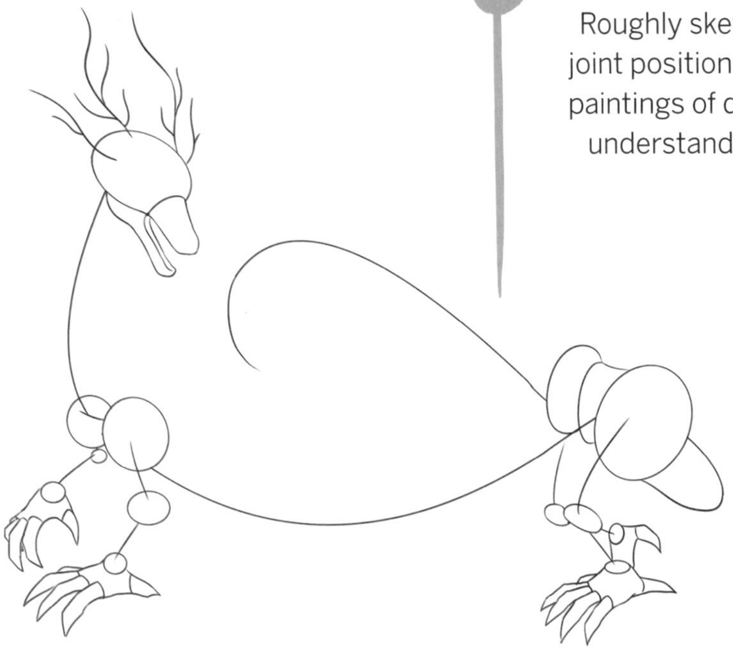

2

As the dragon is 3D, its body should look cylindrical, or rounded, like a sausage. Refine its shape, using curved guidelines, and add detail to its head.

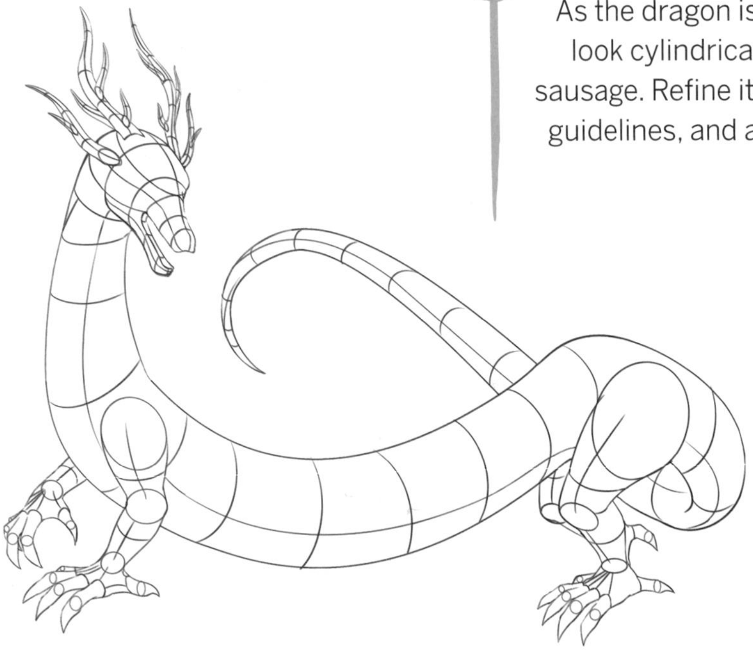

3

Add more detail, sketching the dragon's face, its thick, lustrous mane and iconic fangs. The fangs at the back of the mouth splay outwards slightly.

4

Embellish the mane and add thick, hairy eyebrows. Begin adding scales along the body and fill the mouth with small, sharp teeth.

5

Finish the scales, which look like those on a carp fish, and add detail to its belly. Give your dragon whiskers, a pearl in its claw and some swirly clouds.

ANTHRO TIGER

Ancient sculptures from around 40,000 years ago were found
depicting anthropomorphic (human-like) hybrid creations.
This hybrid character is a cross between a human and a tiger.

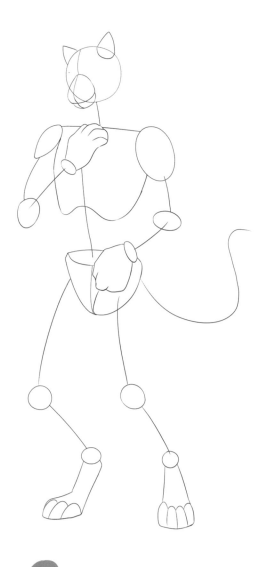

1 Begin with the skeleton and joints. The top half of the body, excluding the head, is human, whereas the legs and feet are those of a tiger.

2 Develop your character's build. Take care over the legs; a tiger walks on its toes with heels raised, unlike a human.

3 What kind of character is this? Sketch your character's face, and then add clothing to suit your character's style.

EXTRA DETAIL

Anthropomorphic characters can take a variety of human-animal forms, for example being part cat, eagle or dog.

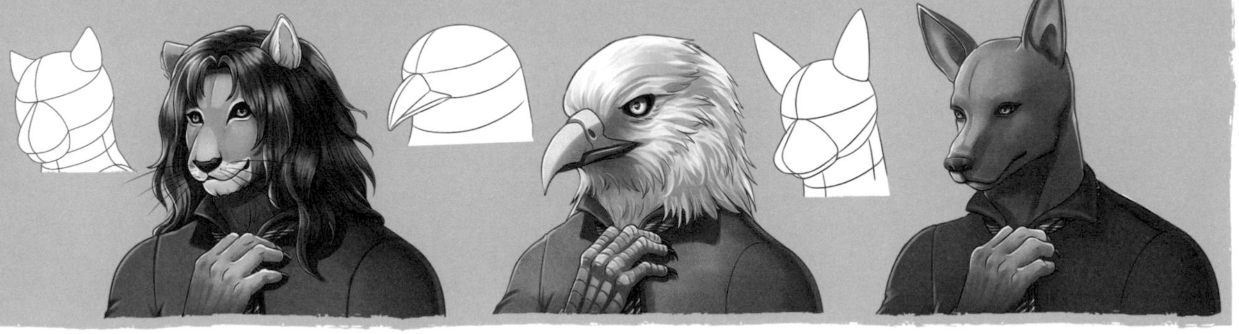

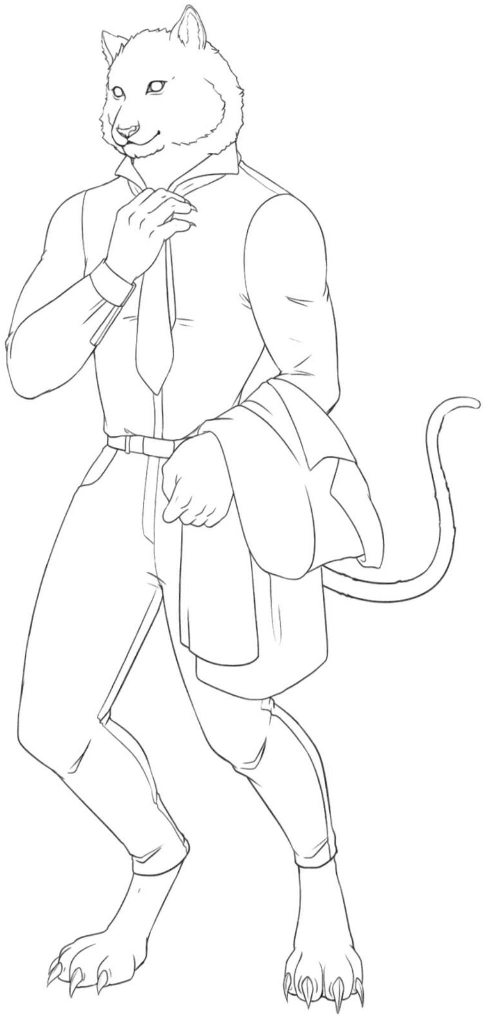

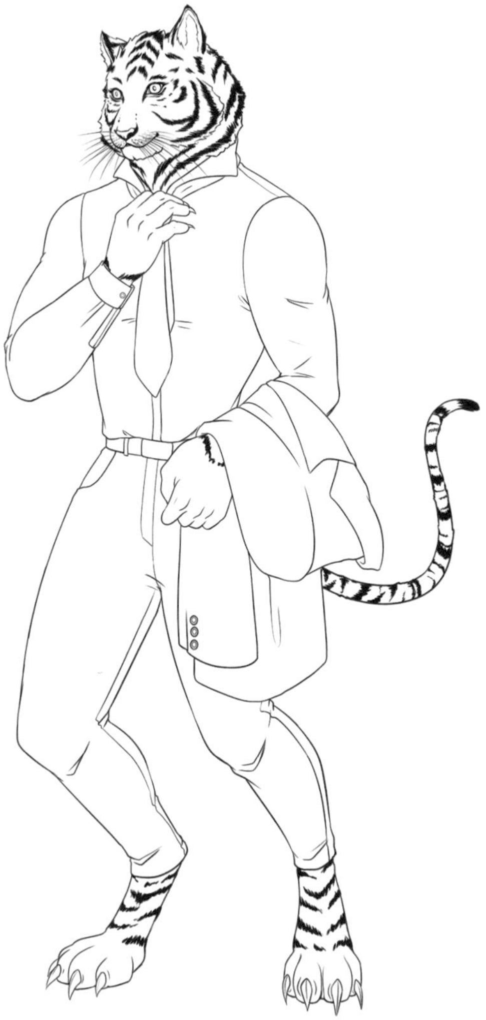

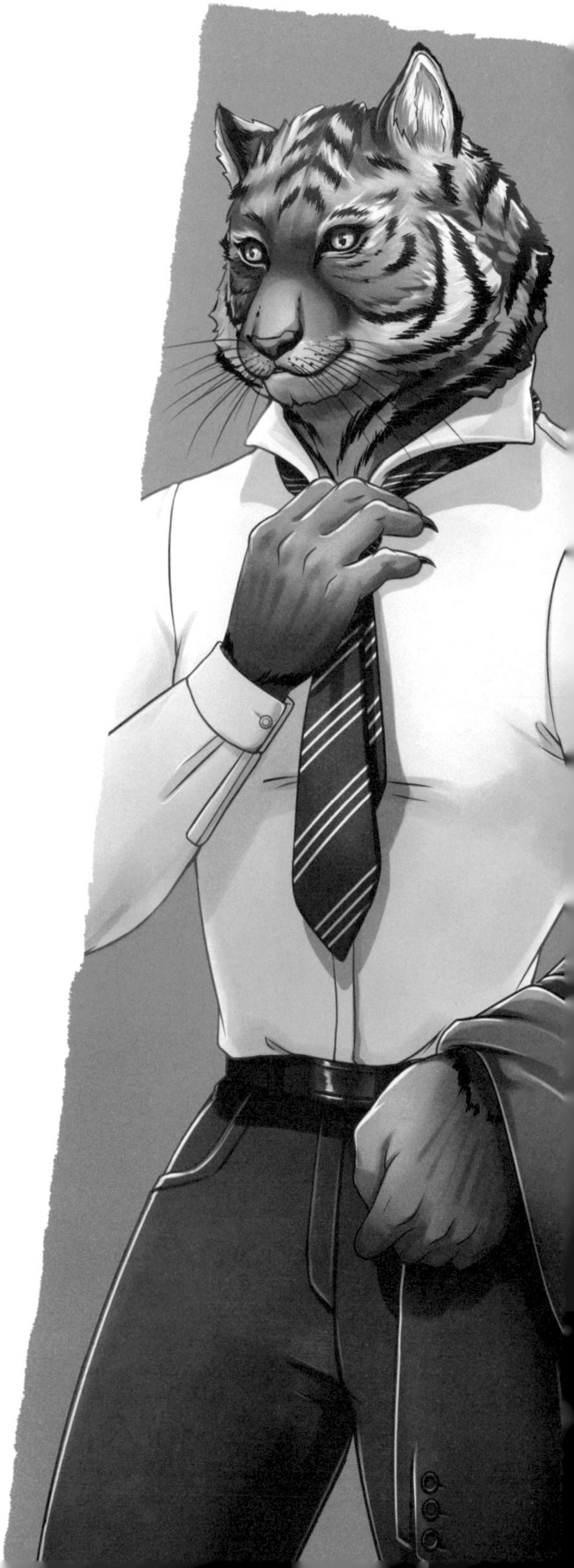

4

Keep adding details, such as tufts of fur, claws, a tie and a jacket thrown over the arm.

5

This anthro's stripes give it away as a human-tiger hybrid. Finish off details such as buttons on the shirt cuffs. Your character could also have tattoos, piercings or jewellery.

HUMAN-MONSTER HYBRID

For a scarier take on human hybrids, try this human-lizard monster akin to a 'lizard-man'. Human-monster hybrids are a popular trope in science fiction and fantasy.

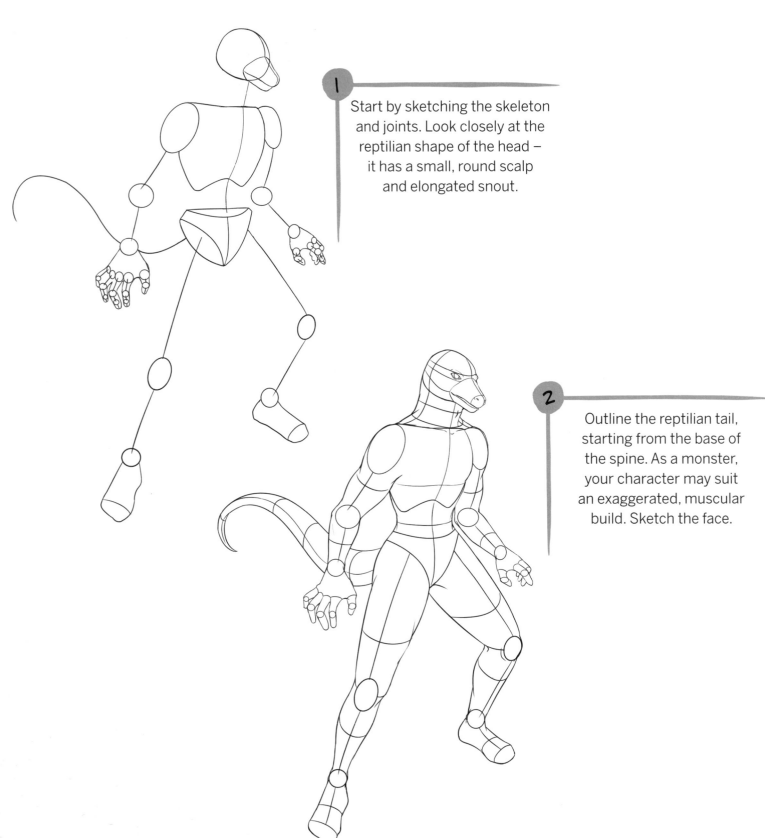

1 Start by sketching the skeleton and joints. Look closely at the reptilian shape of the head – it has a small, round scalp and elongated snout.

2 Outline the reptilian tail, starting from the base of the spine. As a monster, your character may suit an exaggerated, muscular build. Sketch the face.

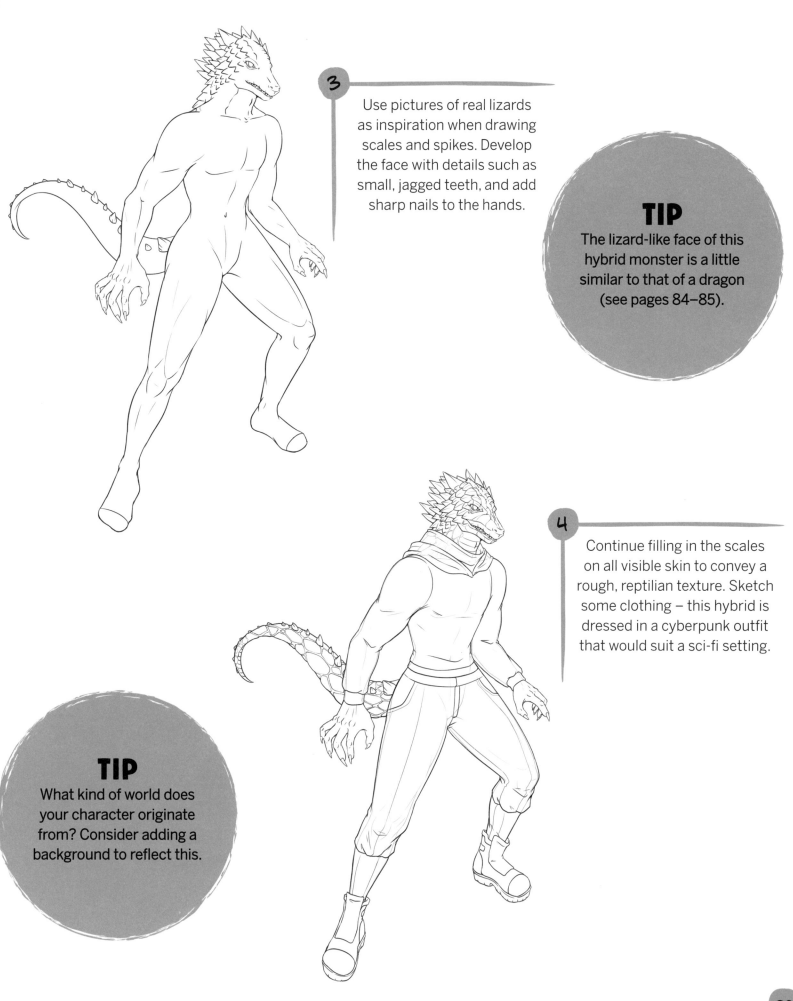

3

Use pictures of real lizards as inspiration when drawing scales and spikes. Develop the face with details such as small, jagged teeth, and add sharp nails to the hands.

TIP
The lizard-like face of this hybrid monster is a little similar to that of a dragon (see pages 84–85).

4

Continue filling in the scales on all visible skin to convey a rough, reptilian texture. Sketch some clothing – this hybrid is dressed in a cyberpunk outfit that would suit a sci-fi setting.

TIP
What kind of world does your character originate from? Consider adding a background to reflect this.

EXTRA DETAIL

The spiky skin texture of your human-monster hybrid should look rough and jagged. Outline each spike individually and add shading to the lower half of each one to give the skin 3D depth.

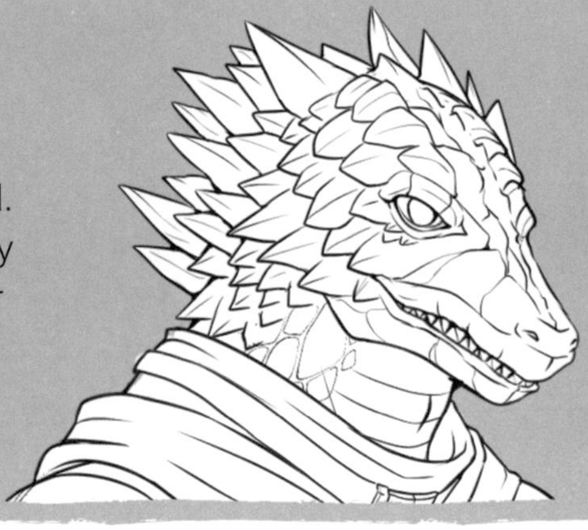

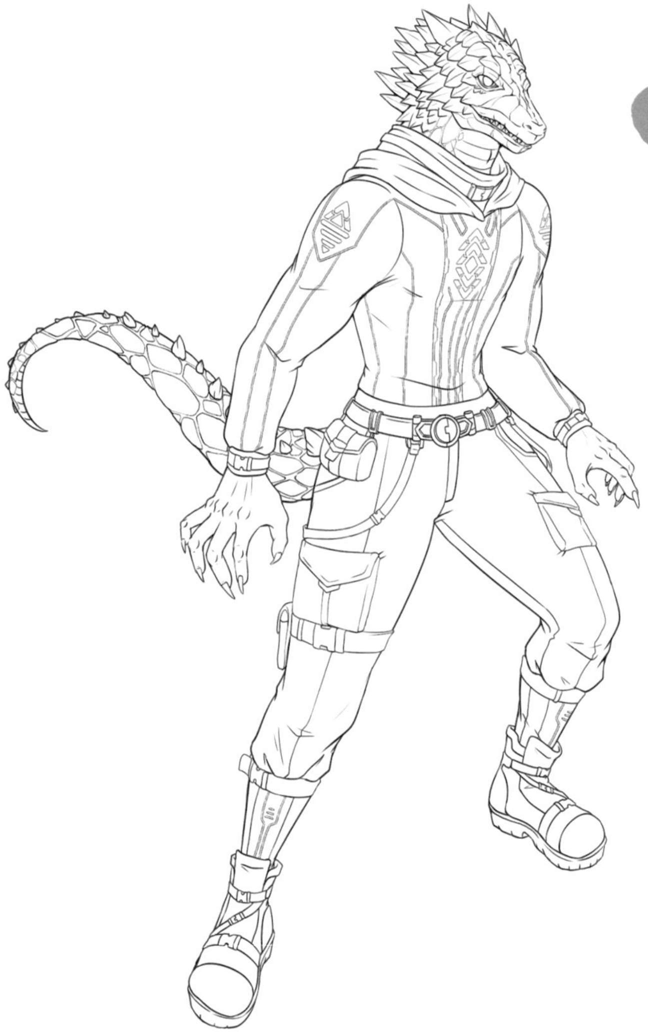

5

Intricate details will make your character appear unique. This monster wears tactical clothing, suggesting its combat skills. What can you add to reveal more about your character?

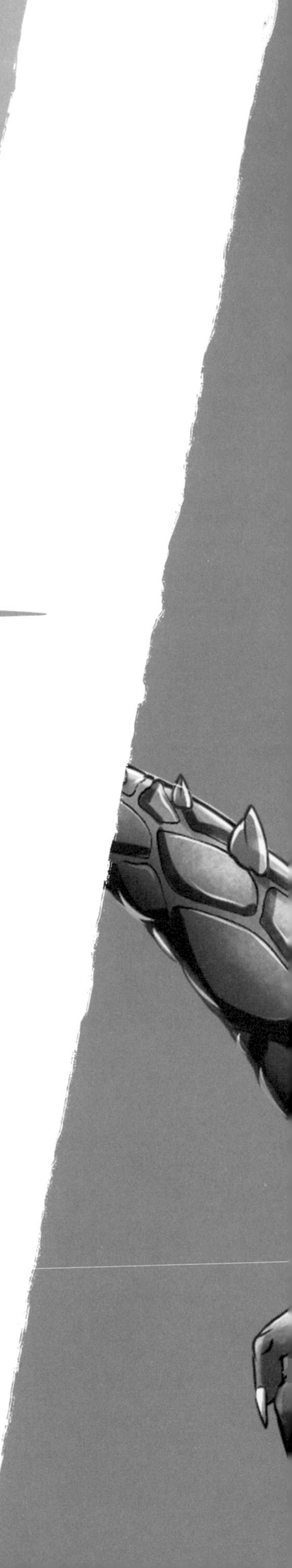

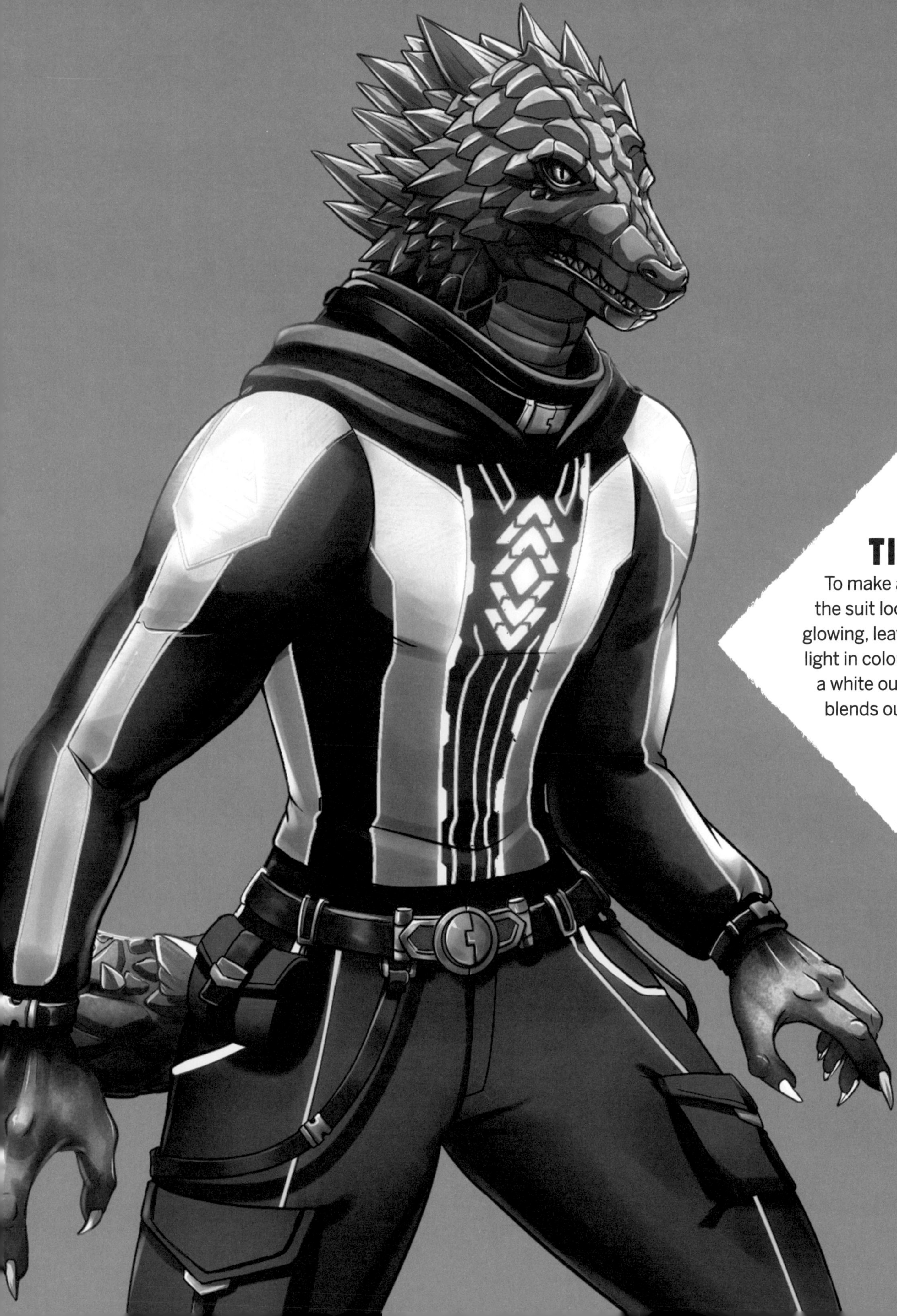

TIP

To make a part of the suit look like it's glowing, leave the area light in colour and add a white outline that blends outwards.

SCI-FI MONSTER

Sci-fi monsters are often based on real-life creatures with exaggerated and distorted proportions. It could be inspired by a single creature or a mixture of animals. Have a go at this monstrous character based on a preying mantis.

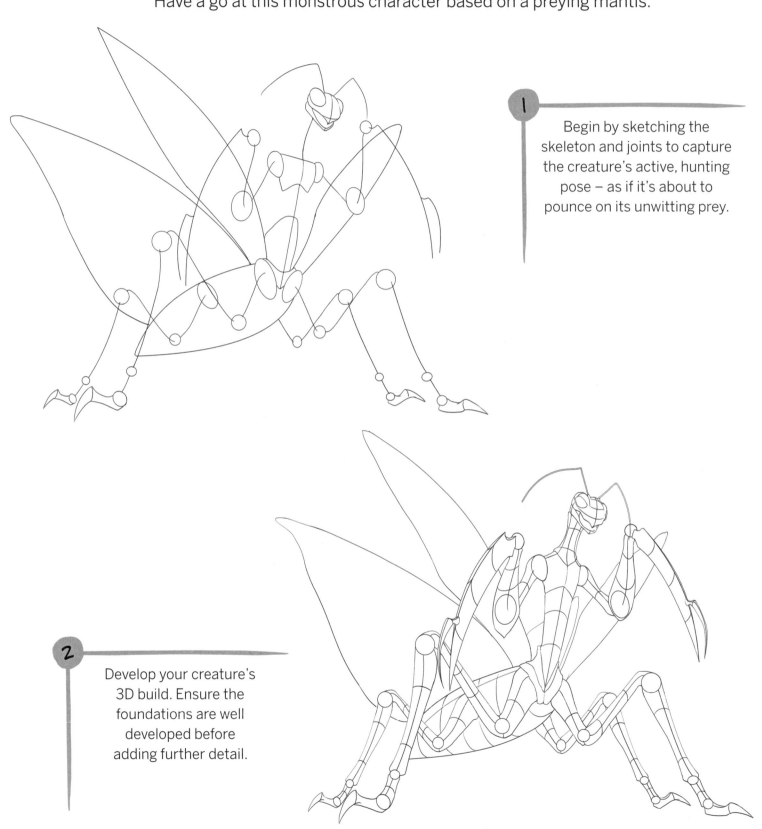

1 Begin by sketching the skeleton and joints to capture the creature's active, hunting pose – as if it's about to pounce on its unwitting prey.

2 Develop your creature's 3D build. Ensure the foundations are well developed before adding further detail.

3

Add eye outlines, sharp teeth and pincers to the face. Begin detailing the segments on the body and spikes down its back.

TIP

When drawing monsters and hybrids based on animals, reference images can help you achieve believable proportions.

4

Continue adding details to make your character menacing. Sketch some veins on the wings to give them texture.

TIP

Enhance your illustration with a high-drama background, and bring it to life with special effects, such as dust and smoke.

5

Focus in on the texture of the body, covering it in jagged spikes to make the surface look coarse and sharp. Add final details to the wings with a light touch, so they look translucent.

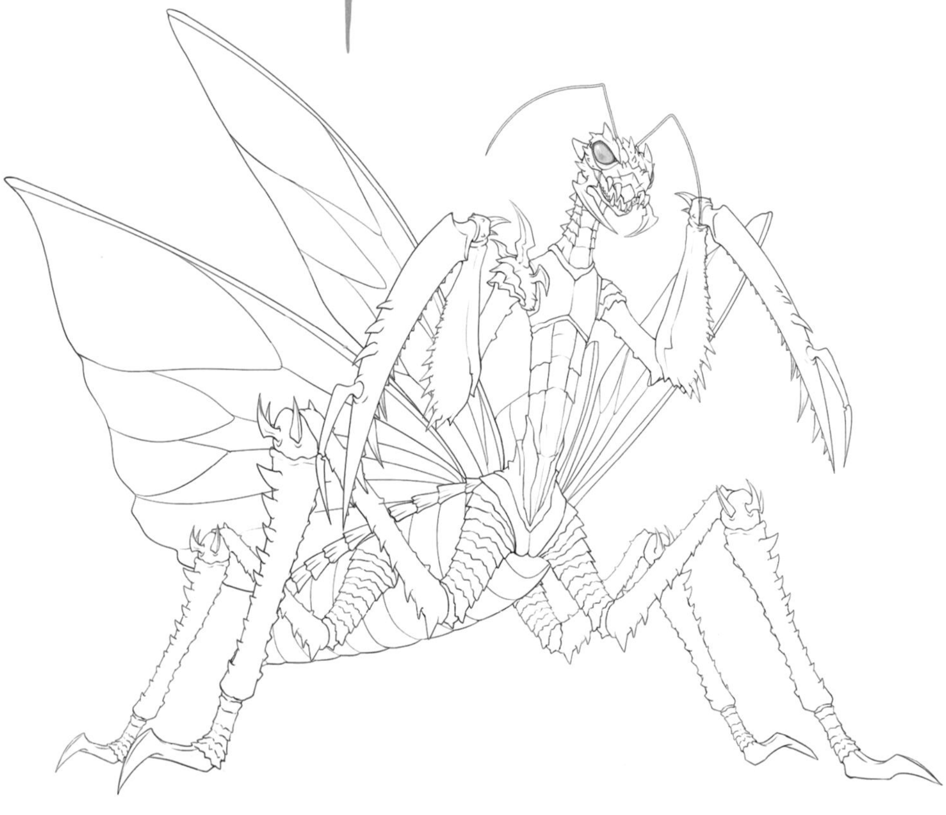

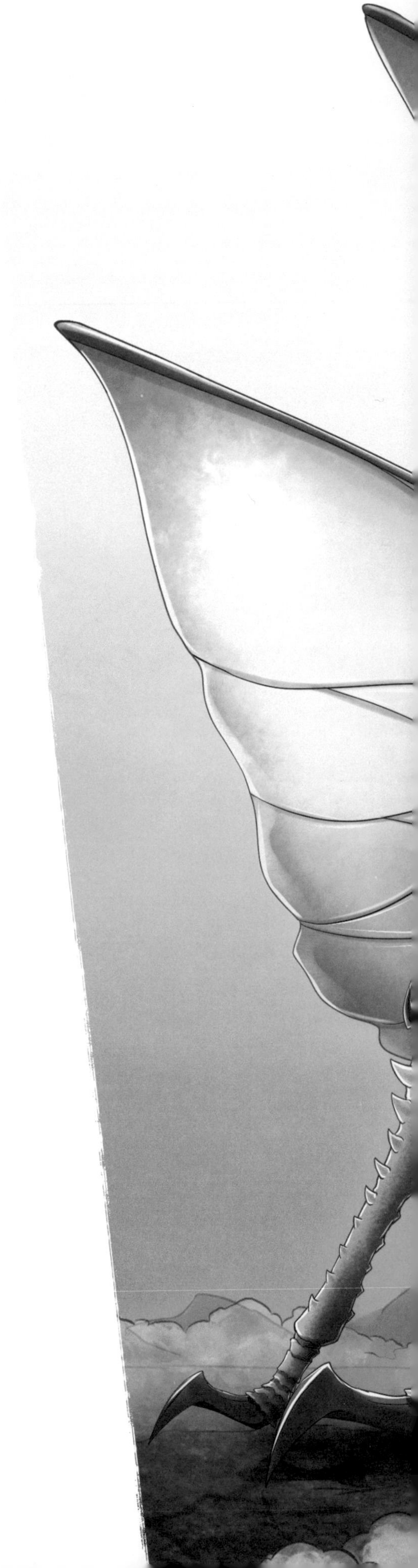

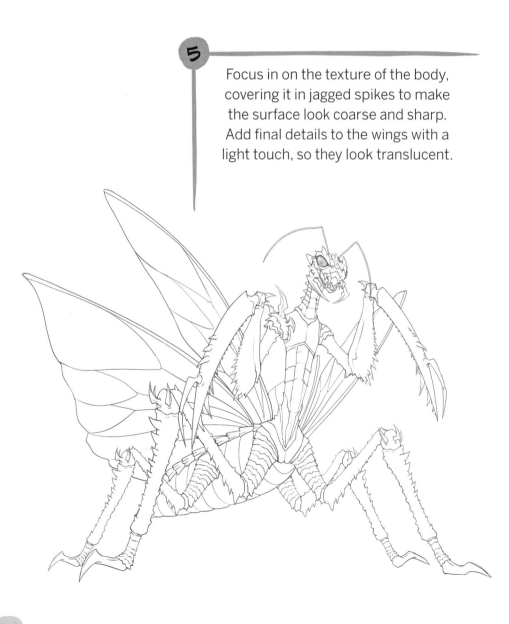

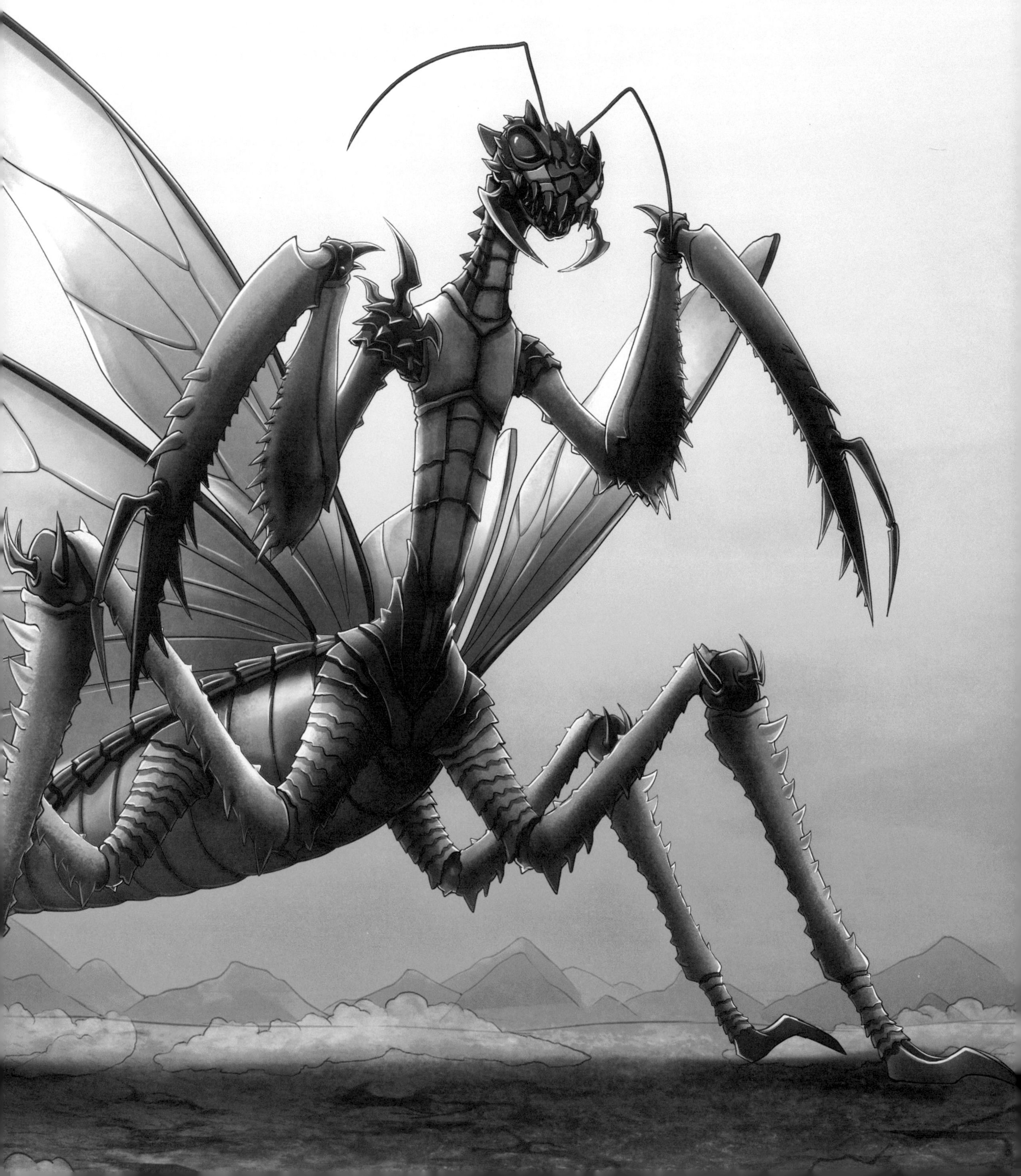

INDEX

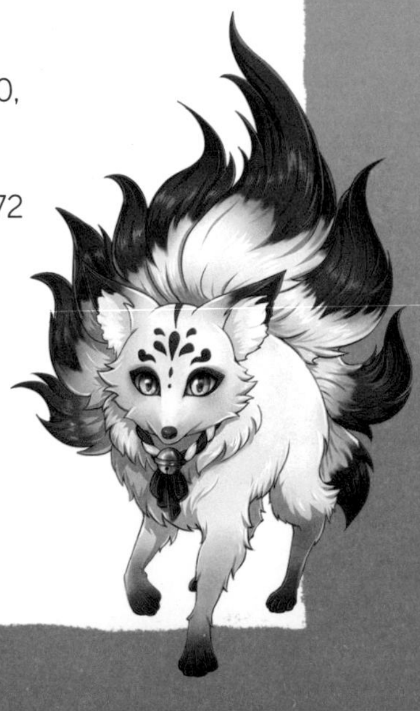